The
Measures
of Success

The Measures of Success

CREATING A HIGH PERFORMING ORGANIZATION

Carl G. Thor

John Wiley & Sons, Inc.

New York · Chichester · Brisbane · Toronto · Singapore

ISBN: 0-471-13180-6

Printed in the United States of America

10 9 8 7 6 5 4 3 2 1

This book is dedicated to my family:
my wife (and business partner), Joyce,
my children, and my parents.
Their support is one thing that is immeasurable.

Contents

Contents

List of Tables
and Figures

Tables

List of Tables and Figures

Figures

List of Tables and Figures

Acknowledgments

This book is mainly the result of the fifteen years I spent at the American Productivity & Quality Center (APQC), where I learned from fellow employees, clients, and partnering organizations of all types. The center's activities were orchestrated by C. Jackson Grayson, Jr., an admitted microeconomic interventionist, who showed me how to become one also.

My early interest in productivity measurement, an obscure specialty at the time, is largely due to patient coaching from John Kendrick and George Sadler. A special thanks goes to a large number of co-instructors of the various APC/APQC courses where we learned about measurement, gainsharing, and benchmarking online. Another special thanks goes to the staff of the APC/APQC library, where I was a major customer over the years, at least in terms of staff time that I required.

I had such good clients at APQC that I often felt more like an editor of their good ideas than their instructor. Most of the examples in the book are hybrids of more than one organization, which is a luxury that experience makes possible. A thanks is also due to Carter Franklin and the students at Houston Baptist University, where I tried out ideas for many years.

I also have learned a great deal from my colleagues in other productivity and quality organizations, and they have provided additional forums for developing my ideas. Most of them come from the Network of Quality and Productivity Centers, the World Confederation of Productivity Sciences, the Shingo Prize for Manufacturing Excellence, and the Quality and Productivity Management

Acknowledgments

Association. A special thanks also goes to the staff of Wheeler Strobel Consulting Group in Australia, where I have done much of my international application. My partner, Joyce Jarrett, gets special mention for her persistence in highlighting the role of the customer, even in places where customer thinking has not been before.

All of this has come together with the people in publishing who make a book like this possible. John Willig first convinced me a book might be feasible. Mary Ann Castronovo Fusco took the jargon and formality that I find natural out of the manuscript and made it into a book that could appeal to anyone, without losing the rigor the subject requires. Jim Childs figured out how to interest you readers, for which I hope you are as grateful as I am.

C.G.T.

Introduction:
You Get What You Measure

If you want to accomplish one thing above all else, a single measure of success can point you toward that goal. If you want frantic action in all directions, give a work group a catalog of two dozen measures, and you probably will see some sort of progress in about half of the less demanding areas. But if you belong to a thoughtful and mature organization, you will want balanced improvement in a handful of measures—five or six selected measures of the key elements of your organization's strategic plan. And you will want everyone who hears about those measures to feel empowered to help with the overall objective of applying them, so that the organization can adapt to changing market forces and succeed.

This book presents measurement as a progressive force in organizational performance improvement. When approached in the manner prescribed in the pages that follow, measurement can align customers' needs and the organization's strategic plan with concerted improvement actions taken by empowered employees at all levels of the organization. Although this book is also intended to serve as a comprehensive guide to the technical aspects of measurement, it is presented in nontechnical language reflecting my nearly twenty years of experience in explaining the overall concepts and specific details of performance measurement to often skeptical audiences around the world.

Introduction

The organization of the book mirrors its readers' varying objectives. The first section—"The Power of Performance Measurement"—outlines a philosophy of measurement as a progressive improvement tool and organizational integrator. This will no doubt appeal to general readers, academicians, and senior executives.

The second and third sections of the book—"Beyond the Bottom Line" and "The Quality Imperative"—deal with choosing the appropriate measures to suit particular situations and offer substantial technical advice. These sections will be most useful to line managers who need to implement measurement systems and to members of their staffs who are unfamiliar with productivity and quality measurement. But this material should also interest the general reader and senior executive charged with directing the implementation of a measurement philosophy in their organization.

The fourth section—"On the Front Line"—provides a thorough introduction to benchmarking and gainsharing, two popular topics that are closely related to measurement and important to its implementation. As its name implies, this section goes on to demonstrate how an organization can develop and use various measures of success. The appendices, glossary, notes, and references at the end of the book encourage further exploration and implementation of the book's ideas.

Five key concepts are woven throughout the twelve chapters of this book:

✿ *Customer needs should be closely related to an organization's strategic plan.* The ultimate tie-breaker on any tough business decision is what the customer really values. In other words, what can the organization effectively give its customers with its current and planned capabilities? This question is just as valid regardless of whether the organization is dealing with internal or external customers.

✿ *There's more to business life than the bottom line.* Of course, profits are vital. But profits are not increased or salvaged by merely meditating on them. They are increased by paying attention to the

Introduction

overall customer concept under which an organization operates and to the day-to-day details of how the work is done. At each level of the organization an appropriately balanced family of measures is needed to create a complete picture of that level's strengths and weaknesses so that appropriate decisions can be made and actions taken.

○ *Constant attention must be paid to consistency of measurement.* For example, when an improvement trend is being measured, the method of calculating baseline and current performance must be *exactly* the same. Although the statement "Consistency is more important than accuracy" may raise a few eyebrows, trend measurers know that consistently calculated approximations (where the source of the inaccuracy is understood) can serve most of an organization's purposes.

○ *Any job or group can be measured.* No one can hide behind the statement, "My work is too complex or variable to be measured." With a little methodological help, anyone who understands the work and its customer environment will be able to measure it.

○ *What is done with the measures is as important as what the measures are.* There are plenty of measures throughout most organizations. The problem is that either the measures are of strategically unimportant factors or the results of the measures are filed away in a drawer for use against occasional senior executive problem-solving forays. Focused development and constant local feedback of a few good measures can be a major motivating and integrating force for the entire organization.

This book can be measured as successful if it

○ Brings a comprehensive approach to measurement to private- and public-sector managers who have neglected measurement or used it too narrowly,

○ Brings some basic technical knowledge on measurement to managers oriented toward behavioral and managerial issues in

Introduction

a manner that suits their behavioral and managerial orientation,

○ Brings some basic behavioral and managerial advice on measurement to managers oriented toward technical issues in a manner that suits their technical orientation,

○ Teaches financial measurement specialists about the usefulness of physical and subjective measures,

○ Teaches productivity specialists oriented toward physical measures about the usefulness of financial and subjective measures,

○ Drives out fear—in this case, concerning the twin specters of operational overcontrol and technical murkiness often associated with measurement,

○ Brings a few good new ideas or even a new way of expressing something to measurement specialists who already know essentially everything in the book, and

○ Provides factory and office workers with a look at a fascinating and important subject they might not otherwise have explored.

Serious readers ought to come away from this book able to understand and participate in the development and use of a comprehensive measurement system in any kind of organization. They will not be armed with all the answers, however, for the only guaranteed generic response in the measurement field is, "It depends." But they will have the proper mind-set and background to work through each issue as it comes up, for they will know how to determine what "it depends" on and how it affects the organization.

Here's to your understanding and development of successful measures of success.

SECTION I

The Power of Performance Measurement

An organization institutes a performance measurement system to stimulate performance improvement. The only way for it to harvest improvement from measured results is to provide those results as feedback to its employees—in the executive suite, on the factory floor, and everywhere in between—who together can make appropriate changes in the processes being measured. What's measured is based on customer needs filtered through a respected strategic plan that reflects organizational capabilities and constraints. At least this is so in a data-driven organization—an organization where management by fact has replaced management by hunch or management by traditional response.

For an organization to be truly data driven, it must consistently gather data from all its levels. Although very different types of measures are used at the top, middle, and bottom of an organization, they must be used with equal persistence. At the top the issues are organizationwide and usually expressed in financial terms. At the bottom, the measures are very specific, typically reflecting local physical counts rather than entries from financial accounting ledgers. At the middle, there's a mixture of these main types of measures. In all cases, the level of the measures should match the span of responsibility of the workers at that level.

Regardless of where they're applied, the measures ultimately selected should be expressed in families—collections of four to six measures tailored to the key planning issues of the level being examined. The goal for the unit doing the measuring should be balanced improvement in all the measures, not a crusade to achieve a stunning victory as reflected by one of the measures.

Ideally, employees at each level meet and reorient their improvement efforts every time a new set of performance results appears. Although their immediate concern is the rate of improvement (trend), they're also working toward a performance level goal that has been thoughtfully set.

Measurement is not a form of after-the-fact accounting. It's the vital online link between customer-driven strategic plans and the current formal improvement efforts of empowered employees at all levels. Measurement provides the driving force to power an organization.

☼ 1 ☼

Tailoring Measures
for Everyone

Something was wrong at XYZ Chemical's largest plant. Although its performance indicators were steady, company executives knew that the plant's financial numbers were flattening at a time when the plant's competitors were showing growth, despite an industrywide inability to raise prices of key products.

Realizing the importance of taking swift action, the plant's operations vice president charged his staff members with assessing the situation. They calculated that a 10 percent reduction in labor costs would lead to enough of an increase in earnings to put the plant on the right track, even if product prices were slow to rise. But they also recognized that the situation warranted additional analysis and managed to obtain a few months to study the problem in more detail before recommending that any workforce reductions be announced.

The staff decided to conduct two performance measurement studies. The first was to break down the plant's profit numbers into two components—productivity and price recovery—to confirm that the productivity problem, which was showing up as an apparent overstaffing, was really there. The second was to look at each support department, where most of the people worked, from the point of view of those departments' internal and external customers to note changes and trends in service requirements.

The results of the studies were astounding—so astounding that management cancelled its original workforce-reduction plans. The staff's investigation revealed that the plant's flat profit performance numbers hid impressive increases in labor productivity and in efficiency of materials and energy usage, which were essentially offset by declines in price recovery (the relation between the price of the product and the unit cost of the inputs for that product). Plant managers were well aware of their inability to raise product prices, but they had not noticed the persistent increase in the prices of most supplies, materials, energy, and even some secondary feedstocks. The most likely forecast called for a leveling of those input costs, combined with a gradual increase in the final product price. Thus, continued productivity improvement would eventually drive profitability up.

The study group also identified four key support groups, which felt they were appropriately staffed. The members of each group asked themselves the following questions: "What does the group do? Who are its customers? What do they want? How much time is spent reaching the customers' desired outcome? How much of the remaining work actually adds value?"

In general, the departments found themselves to be surprisingly off target in much of their work. Their customers often needed much less "stuff," but some of what they needed had to be provided more quickly or more accurately. As for staffing the support groups, one department needed a few additional people to do its job well and one department had the right amount of workers, but the other two could be cut 30 to 40 percent. The net effect was a little more than a 10 percent reduction—not the 10 percent across-the-board reduction that was originally planned.

XYZ Chemical learned several lessons from this experience. For starters, having top management concentrate on the bottom line is not enough. Profitability data need to be broken down and their components analyzed. The work of every part of the organization needs to be directed toward the outcomes desired by its customers.

Tailoring Measures for Everyone

Useful measurement involves several measures, not just those that focus on cost or quantity. Feedback from customer to supplier can lead to the kind of performance improvements that technical experts dream about. In XYZ's case, intelligent use of performance measures prevented a serious strategic mistake and inspired company managers to properly redirect their efforts and apply this approach throughout the organization. A small amount of judicious measurement not only altered this chemical firm's immediate fate, but also institutionalized a program that its managers can tap to determine the right road to follow whenever they find themselves at a critical crossroad.

The Many Faces of Measurement

As we have just seen, measurement is useful at all levels of an organization but is handled quite differently in each place. Like beauty, measurement is in the eye of the beholder. An organization as a whole performs in a different arena than a division or department, which is different from a small work group or individual. Moreover, performance is much more than the direct effect of human labor. Individuals may decide how various resources will be used, but measurable changes can show up in a variety of guises— from less use of energy for the same work to lower levels of inventory for the same sales.

At the top of an organization, the measurement horizon is long: it can stretch anywhere from the next quarter to the next decade. Typically, top management's main question is, "Are we on plan?" or, "Do we need to modify our plan to consider a new insight?" The focus does not stray very far from profitability, and the language used to express top management concerns is financial, but consideration is given to major customer demands, market share, and organizational image. Because of the complexity or generality of the measures at this level, the measured results require further interpretation before corrective action can be taken.

Everything is exactly the opposite for work groups on the factory floor and for front-line representatives in a service organization. The normal time frame for measurement ranges from minute-to-minute to this week. "Are we on plan?" (or "Am I on plan?") is still the principal issue, but the plan in question is more likely to be this hour's plan rather than a ten-year plan. The language used here is physical: units, pounds, inches, minutes, components. There isn't enough time to compute the worth of these outputs in dollars, even if doing so would be useful. *Control* is the watchword. Measurement is frequent or even automatically continuous. There is little ambiguity about the measured results: the unit count is enough or not enough; the specifications are met or not met; the cause of deviation is either obvious or can be determined by conferring with other team members, a supervisor, or the internal customer.

In the middle of an organization, there is, not surprisingly, a middling type of measurement that can best be described as screening or diagnosis. The scope involves much more than a single machine or work station but does not encompass a whole division or department. The time frame for measurement ranges from this week to this quarter, but much of it is done month by month. The data may be both financial (related to cost) and physical (related to such factors as time and waste). Such well-known quality-improvement tools as Pareto analysis, fishbone charts, and flow-charting may be used to obtain insight at this level, but expert help is rarely required.

Regardless of where performance measures are taken, they have to tie into the organization's strategic plan and address its customers' concerns. Typically an organization's strategic plan provides direction and indicates how resources will be divided. It's natural for everyone to want profitability, market share, quality products and services, timely customer service, happy employees, large dividends, a strong community image, earnings growth, new products and services, and even a winning company softball team. In theory, these can all be obtained together. But in reality, an organization will tend to lead in some areas and lag behind in others. Therefore, priorities must be set and tradeoffs made. The plan helps the organi-

Tailoring Measures for Everyone

zation's leaders make these tough decisions by requiring them to focus on the organization as a whole. As the plan is rolled out to lower levels of the organization, it helps focus each successive department, group, and business process on obtaining the organization's objectives.

Priorities will be set according to stakeholders' interests. The external customer of the organization would like on-time delivery of a late-model product or service that not only works but also is fairly priced. The stockholders would like excellent profit margins, earnings growth, and various forms of stability. The employees (internal customers of each other) want high wages, good working conditions, few hassles, and community esteem. Regulators simply want less smoke coming out of the chimneys. All these groups are "customers" and must be considered in an organization's strategic plan. Therefore, saying that an organization must prepare a customer-driven strategic plan doesn't narrow things down very much.

What does narrow things down in a disciplined organization is the type of performance measure that is chosen and reviewed at each level. To a large degree, this is the power of performance measurement, for you get what you measure. "Which customer is attended to first? Which investment gets funded first? Which process gets reengineered first? What is the design team concentrating on?" The choice of measures is true bottom line. As the eminent economic historian Witold Kula has noted, "The right to determine measures is an attribute of authority in all civilized societies."[1] Measuring body count or throw weight gets you people looking urgently for more body count or throw weight.

Thus, when it's time for an organization to select its measures, the question of what is the "right" measure is not a technical question to which there is a single answer. The real question is, "What do we want to have happen in this time period if we can concentrate on only a few things?" And the right measure is the one that tells an organization's managers whether those critical things are happening.

Performance measurement is not limited to a particular type of industry or size of organization. Measurement is for everyone. In general, you measure the most important things that are (or should be) happening to determine whether they are occurring as planned. Ideally, an organization's plans are driven by customer needs and interests. For example, manufacturers are concerned with the level of output of their product and its quality and costs. Something identifiable is being produced at an identifiable cost for an identifiable customer. In service industries or government agencies, the products and customers may not be as obvious, but they, too, can be identified. Social service agencies handle cases, think tanks conduct studies, and creative groups generate ideas. Within an organization, the "customer" is often the next work station—an internal customer, but nevertheless a customer whose needs are important. When a group of any size asserts that it has nothing to measure, it puts itself in danger of being branded unnecessary. Every group performs by doing something for a customer.

Measures at Every Step of the Process

Performance measurement is most closely associated with the attainment of strategic objectives. If organizations' strategic thinking were always dominated by customer-related concerns, if planning were truly rolled out to all points of the organization so that it involved everyone, and if "act" always followed "plan" as it does in the textbooks, measurement would be very easy. Attainment of plan would be everyone's starting and ending point for the selection of measures.

Many organizations do a good job of assessing customer needs through surveys, special teams, and even electronic networking. But measuring customers' feelings about how their needs are being met is only part of the equation. An excellent organization will strive to meet customers' needs even when—and especially when—customers are not carefully monitoring the goods and services they receive. It is necessary to measure the "facts" of the relationship in addition to the perceptions.

Tailoring Measures for Everyone

Long-term strategic objectives are set by putting customer input data together with organizational capabilities, constraints, and intentions. A basic balance is created between a large number of desirable things. Some high-priority items will be handled immediately, while items assigned a lower priority will be postponed or avoided. The customer is still always right, but every issue can't be addressed instantly.

In the short run, the appropriate level of the organization must take corrective action on an immediate concern, such as a poorly handled customer. If the strategic plan has been rolled out to that level, a clear set of priorities will be in place, and the matter will be settled appropriately. Measurement systems can monitor that response and provide information that the organization can use to review the basic priorities and procedures, if needed.

Measures of customer service quality and satisfaction vary not only according to organizational level but also from industry to industry. Virtually everyone measures on-time delivery and whether a product or service works as specified. Customers usually are also concerned with price and cost, order-cycle time (how long it took from entering the order to receiving the product or service), and such postdelivery issues as maintainability and documentation. Organizations that want to satisfy their customers and attract new ones also must keep this fundamental question in mind: "Is our current product or service really good enough, or is it time to design something better?"

To satisfy a customer at the point of delivery—the so-called moment of truth—an organization needs to do a great deal of work out of sight of the customer, or upstream. Organizations must also measure this upstream performance, so they can supplement the customer's perception with their own reality checks. Some of the things being measured are the same as the customer measures— price and cost, on-time delivery, cycle times, whether it works. But the measurement occurs at an intermediate point in the production process as well as at the end. In addition, there are other measures, such as labor productivity (output per hour); first-pass yield (how often the product was produced or the service delivered right the first time); rework hours; scrap and other tangible waste; inventory levels; waiting time; energy, supplies, and equipment use; process variation; and even team effectiveness and morale, which give insight into interrelated aspects of the upstream processes that should lead to even better final delivery. Each of these types of measures has its own story and will be discussed in depth later in this book.

Besides being technically well designed and comprehensive, a performance measurement system must be understood and used properly by everyone in each part of the organization. Feedback is the lubrication that keeps the measurement system running smoothly. Measured results should be promptly given to the responsible party with an explicit mandate to improve the situation, within broad policy guidelines. In this way, measurement becomes an effective tool instead of an elaborate but rarely used program.

Feedback will be mainly between an external customer and the designated contact person, and then between that contact person and the appropriate operating group or groups. Although internal customer problems may be more complex, interorganizational feedback is typically horizontal. Ideally, feedback travels vertically, up the organization's chain of command, only when there is disagreement or neglect in the horizontal communication. In an effective organization, feedback doesn't require "defending" one's actions. Facts are presented and interpreted and actions are taken with the aim of getting the job done swiftly and effectively. Later, the mistakes that were found can be discussed. When it comes to feedback, the cliché that "there is no limit on what can be accomplished if no one cares who gets the credit" certainly holds true. Similarly, great strides can be made if little attention is paid to who is to "blame" for an error, as long as efforts to avoid finger pointing do not cover up a defect in the process or system that can be corrected.

The manner in which feedback is given and received can be as important as the actual content.[2] The best operational feedback is given personally by the responsible party to the whole relevant group in a setting where open communication is encouraged. Even when those receiving the feedback include people from outside the organization, straightforward personal discussion is best. Once that format becomes standard, it is possible to supplement full feedback with periodic bulletin-board flyers, charts, and reports on relatively noncontroversial issues. But unless the measurement system is humanized with regular and candid face-to-face communication, it will never be effective.

The Challenge of Measurement

Opponents of measurement have been around since at least the first century. When the concept of bushel was introduced into the grain trade, the ancient Jewish statesman and historian Flavius Josephus worried about "measures, an innovation that changed a world of innocent and noble simplicity into one forever filled with dishonesty."[3] Centuries later, the sole experience of many modern managers with measurement remains with manipulated budgets and petty job ratings and performance appraisals.

When managers aren't trained in proper measurement, measurement techniques can overwhelm or, even worse, stupefy. As it's been noted, the first four letters of the word *number* do spell *numb*.[4] But most of the time, a highly technical approach to measurement isn't necessary or even appropriate. If the person or group being measured understands and "owns" the measure as much as they "own" their job, the measure will become a normal part of getting the job done well.

When measurement fails, it's usually because the measurers and their supervisors don't have a clear idea of why they're measuring in the first place. The goal of measurement is to stimulate customer-driven improvement—nothing more and nothing less. And since the path to improvement is different in each organization, each measurement path will also be unique.

Measurement in and of itself does not cause improvement. But the right kind of measurement opens up an organization to self-analysis. An organization that measures itself well will tend to have

○ Lower processing costs,

○ Quicker response time to customers,

○ More demanding product and service standards,

○ Bolder, more confident employees,

○ Better process integration, both internally and with suppliers,

○ A greater ability to challenge fixed overhead costs, and

○ A clearer plan for the future.

In their drive to obtain these payoffs through comprehensive measurement, organizations need the kind of leadership that stresses openness and flexibility and that quickly provides any needed resources. In short, they need a breed of leaders who understand that the cost of getting to know their organization and its customers is never too high.

☼ 2 ☼

Building a Family
of Measures

"How's your family?" You've probably been asked that question countless times. And chances are, unless something extraordinary was going on or had recently occurred—a birth, a death, a new job, a wedding, a graduation, a promotion—you probably answered that question with a simple, "Just fine, thanks." The simplicity of that response, however, belies the complexity of the question.

If your family happens to be doing something together at the time the question is asked, there is an obvious collective answer. During a family cross-country vacation, for example, everyone is in the same car, going to the same place, on the same time schedule. The family is "fine" or "not fine" together. But even when the family is engaged in a collective activity, such as a family vacation, some family members are doing "better" than others, and any attempt to judge the overall family well-being becomes a rough and weighted approximation.

Not only are the different family members faring differently for any given variable—for example, some are hungry, some are not—but they each have their own separate set of important concerns. With a vacationing family, the father may be mainly concerned with arriving at the hotel on schedule. A secondary but nonetheless important consideration for him may be adequate meals. The mother may be primarily interested in photographing unusual rock formations en route to the destination. A secondary but important interest for her might be the children's behavior. The son may be mainly interested in adequate meals and secondarily interested in expanding his beer-signs-seen list. The daughter may be mainly interested in being the first to locate new rock formations or beer signs and secondarily interested in listening to her Walkman.

"So how is this vacationing family?" To answer that question, you can ask each member and tally their responses. Or you can find some common general themes to evaluate, such as

○ Logistics (schedule attainment and adequacy of meals),

○ Sufficiency of target stimuli (rock formations and beer signs), and

○ Overall atmosphere (how everyone is getting along in the car).

If the family had done some predeparture strategic planning, these might have been the priorities they would have chosen. Each individual probably would have articulated them a little differently, but there would, no doubt, be some overlapping requirements: family members tend to share interests and would probably be amenable to making certain compromises—for example, agreeing to fall behind schedule a bit if it meant getting to see a new and unusual rock formation. But the fundamental unit of measurement is the individual member of the family.

This becomes apparent when the family returns from vacation. Then the various family members have their own job or school, friends, and physical space in addition to their own personal health. Nonetheless, when someone asks, "How's the family?" the answer still remains a weighted average of an implicit set of measures for each family member reflecting separate but occasionally related issues. Thus, the family's overall well-being can be tabulated in two ways:

1. *By individual.* Father is fine, mother is OK, son is unhappy, daughter is ecstatic. Thus, the family is about average.

Building a Family of Measures

2. *By issue.*   The job and school are fine, friends are OK, physical space is cramped and messy, health is excellent. Thus, the family is about average.

In short, to assess the family's well-being, you must determine a balance in their lives. You must study not just the father or the mother, the son or the daughter, but each of them separately and collectively. And so it is with any group or organization. To determine how well an organization is functioning, its leaders must not restrict their focus to just one indicator—one individual, one department, one product, one process, one expenditure, one measure of success. They must examine an entire family of measures.

Any organization moves along a path that is the result of a collection of various influences and pressures. For example, an organization must be responsive to its external customers. But which external customers? One wants a lower-priced product; another wants a more capable version. One wants elaborate packaging; another wants bulk shipment. One wants truckload deliveries; another wants bicycle-load deliveries. In addition, there are other external customers or stakeholders—owners and the community, for instance—who are more final-outcome oriented. Those stakeholders don't necessariliy care how the organization reaches its goals—that is, what they perceive its goals to be—as long as the organization increases its earnings per share, decreases effluents, keeps employment up, or whatever is of primary concern to them. A progressive organization will also want to satisfy its internal customers—to have smooth and intelligent relations between the different parts of the organization and within its key processes.

Only a family of measures can help an organization strike the balance needed to satisfy its external and internal customers. Since there is no single bottom line that satisfies all requirements, a reasonable amount of progress is needed on several diferent fronts. Sometimes it is possible to weight the conflicting requirements, so that some are given more importance than others. For example, a factory faced with the possibility of having to shut down will want to give high weight to significant and speedy improvement in market share and low weight to a moderate reduction in effluents over the course of the year.

Even when handling issues where there is no conflict between different customers, a work group must address several variables. A supervisor may ask for reduced defects, more product output, and more training investment from the work group. Weighting these requirements will help the group formulate its production plans.

Locking in on a clear definition of the desired balance may seem difficult, but once that balance is in place, the work units can run smoothly. They are spared the "today's theme" oscillation that is so typical of the traditional hierarchical organization trying to manage with a single bottom-line indicator. Such a narrow focus can lead to situations where an assembly line speeds up to increase output, then slows down to reduce defects, and then stops altogther while the workers attend a training class, rework defects, or wait for supervisory clarification. It's not by accident that continuous improvement through total quality management has become such a popular goal. Discontinuity is the enemy of balance. Continuity in plans, improvements, and customer relations requires balance in measurement as expressed in families of measures.

The Characteristics of a Family of Measures

There is a surprising number of factors to consider when designing a family of measures. To be effective, the measures must have the following seven characteristics.

1. The family of measures must be linked to the appropriate level of the strategic plan and expressed in that level's language.

Every division, department, work group, and individual works and thinks using a unique language. "I want you to handle that" can

Building a Family of Measures

mean anything from "Let's hide this in your drawer instead of mine" to "Tell me how you solved the problem by tomorrow morning."

Similarly, before you can tackle a particular measure, such as "Problems solved per month," you must first make sure that everyone understands certain key words. *Problems* can be difficult to define but might be identified through the use of an activity log and a weighting system. *Solved* is difficult to define because sometimes you can't tell whether a problem truly has been resolved until much later, even years later.

Tailoring the members of a family of measures to fit a particular usage would be fairly easy if the only people using the measures were locals—that is, those in a specific department, office, or region being measured or those handling the specific process, product, or service being measured. But these measures are also occasionally used for upward feedback in the organization. Therefore, they must also be meaningful to bosses and bosses' bosses, as well as to external customers and observers. The measures must reflect the strategic threads that run vertically through the organization.

If the top of the organization says productivity is important and should be monitored everywhere, each family of measures will probably have a member or two that represents productivity. At the top of the organization, the output side of productivity might be some financial aggregate, such as value added; at the top level of a factory, the output might be physical tons or units shipped; at the section level, it might be tons melted or cases shipped; in a support group, it might be reports finished or entries made. In each case, much explaining and defining can be expected when a measure leaves its locality—that is, its place of origin. But it is critical to maintain the strategic thread of productivity as a vital indicator throughout the organization. This also applies to other strategic threads, such as quality, customer satisfaction, timeliness, and innovation. Each means very different things in different parts of the organization, but many organizations would want to ensure that one or more of these strategic threads is reflected everywhere in the organization. The challenge, in a nutshell, is to successfully decentralize an intentionally centralizing strategic concept.

2. The family of measures must be well communicated throughout the organization.

No matter how carefully a family of measures is crafted, if it isn't well communicated throughout the organization, the work that went into creating those measures is all for nothing. Communication must not only be made but also received. And, as the following case illustrates, managers must learn not to underestimate the amount of information that their workers can absorb and understand.

One major chemical company installed a plantwide measurement system as part of a gainsharing plan, which is a form of performance-driven group incentive. From the beginning, the project was a joint venture between management and the local union, and they worked together for many months selecting and finetuning the measures. At first there was some apprehension among management that opening the books to the union might lead to difficulties, even though the "books" in question were the operating books, not the financial ledgers. Older management members believed that union members wouldn't be able to' understand the numbers, so there would be no problem. But some of the newer managers felt that a partial understanding of the information would lead to difficulties at bargaining time.

In fact, on viewing the newly released data, a few of the union workers were able to combine accounting skills, which had been derived from outside interests, with a deep knowledge of the plant's operations, derived from personal experience with the plant and its physical indicators. The measurement system that the management-union committee developed was launched successfully and became a model for measurement programs in other organizations. When the company made presentations about its measurement system and gainsharing plan, it sent a two-person team made up of a manager, who introduced the generalities and discussed the policy implications of the plans, and a union member, who presented the technical details and answered computational questions.

Building a Family of Measures

As this experience shows, understanding can be stretched. Never assume that people won't be able to understand something, especially if there is sufficient motivation for them to want to understand. Employees will be receptive to the technical aspects of the family of measures approach *if*

- ✪ The approach has been accepted in principle by those who will be covered by it, and

- ✪ They know that they will help develop the measurement system.

3. The family of measures must be made up of enough members to ensure completeness but not so many that the organization loses its focus.

A family of measures should have between four and six members. Although families of three and even families of fifteen or twenty have been created and used, they typically have less success than those that focus on four to six indicators. It is rare for any group or process to be simple enough to be captured in only one to three measures. On the other hand, directing effort toward improvement requires focus. It is practically impossible to focus on fifteen or twenty things at the same time, especially if those things are subtle and overlap. The six-measure maximum stems from the simple observation that six measures are about all that the average person can remember without notes. (Notes shouldn't be required when talking about the focus of your work life!)

Over a period of several years, some of the measures may be changed, so that more than six things end up being analyzed. But six is enough at any one time. Most work processes require individuals to consider productivity and cost, quality and effectiveness, timeliness, and something else that is specific to the situation, such as safety, documentation, or innovation.

4. The family of measures must be technically sound.

Measures must accurately gauge the process, department, or what-ever else is being measured. Therefore, the members of the family need to be expressed clearly. What is entitled "units per hour" may, in fact, be "weighted units per paid hour." Weighting is discussed in greater detail later in this book, but there may be "large" and "small" units that require different amounts of labor. Weighting would give extra credit for the larger units to guard against an uncontrollable product mix change being mistaken for productivity improvement. Hours could be hours paid, hours present, or hours actually work-ing. Since each gives a different story, scrupulous consistency is required to ensure accurate tracking of any trends.

Each measure needs a baseline, or starting point. Where a mea-sure has been showing steady improvement historically, the result for the latest time period is usually a good base. Curve A in Figure 2.1 shows rapid improvement in output per hour—from 15 units per hour at the beginning of year 1992 to 19 units per hour in 1994. For 1995 it's reasonable to expect at least a continuation of the 19 units per hour rate.

Where there has been much fluctuation, some kind of average may be better. Curve B shows a performance range of 12.2 to 16.0 units per hour with an average observation over the three years of about 14.6. Thus, 14.6 might be the best base to use in such an uncertain situation.

Sometimes there is even a "normal" concept that can be applied, based on a machine or labor standard or some other conventional expectation. Curve C shows the manufacturer's "suggested stan-dard" to be 11 units per hour.

The relative importance of each of the members of the family needs to be expressed if there is a desire to be able to report or use an overall measure of the balanced family. This determination is also called *weighting*. The rule of thumb on family weighting is that no single member should get more than 50 percent or less than 10 percent of the weight. More than 50 percent would make a single

Building a Family of Measures

FIGURE 2.1. EXAMPLES OF MEASURED RESULTS

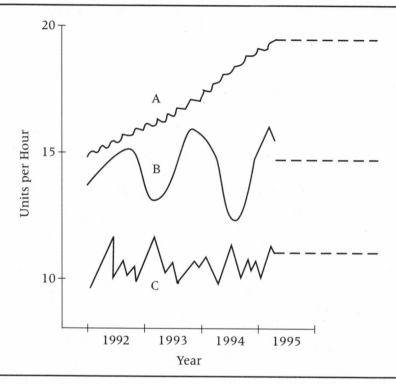

measure so important that no one would pay attention to the other family members. If there is a single measure that seems to merit such a high rating, it is usually because it has been expressed too generally or inclusively. It should be split into two measures, each with a more modest weight. This will generate data that are more precise and useful.

A less than 10 percent weight would consign a member to oblivion. This type of measure can still be calculated and reviewed by specialists, but it should not clutter up the main focus of the family of measures. The weight is not intended to state what is most important, but rather to help the organization focus on what needs to be addressed in the next time period. Safety frequently gets a 10 percent weight. If the level of safety practice is poor, safety is the "most important" measure. But if the organization routinely enjoys a high level of safety, it can be deemphasized as an immediate focus without implying that it is "not important."

5. The family of measures must be taken and reviewed as often as appropriate.

Since the purpose of measurement is to help make improvement happen, the frequency of measurement depends on how often it is appropriate to intervene in improvement. On the factory floor, control measures might be taken every minute because the relevant machine is capable of nearly instant readjustment. The individual members of a family of measures for a factory floor team might be summarized every day for review, and the balanced family might be reviewed once a week.

At the upper levels of a department or division or in a marketing or purchasing support area, individual family measures might be compiled weekly, and the balanced family reviewed every two weeks or every month. Here the unit of detailed thinking is a week at a time, and policy shifts might occur as often as monthly. There is no need to provide new measures every day because instructions to employees are issued on a weekly basis.

At the top of the entire organization, individual measures would usually be taken no more often than monthly, with the aggregated family of measures assessed less frequently—for example, quarterly, when general results are reported to stockholders. In an exceptional case where a special program is being run, measures might be taken weekly, but major corporate programs usually cannot afford that many checkpoints.

6. The family of measures must provide information on both level and trend.

Performance measurement has recently become associated with continuous improvement—that is, at what rate the measured entity is improving. For example, output per person hour increased

Building a Family of Measures

2.3 percent this quarter, after averaging 1.9 percent for the past two years. Or on-time delivery has improved from 87.3 percent three years ago to 94.1 percent this month.

In many management circles, continuous improvement is equated with slow or gradual improvement. While a steady annual improvement rate of 5 percent over five years might initially look good on paper, if this improvement trend results only in the organization going from a horrible level of performance to a fair level of performance, that organization needs more than gradual improvement. It needs breakthrough improvement.

An intelligent organization searches for improvement that will add value to the customer. Clearly the preference is for breakthroughs—when those breakthroughs are both timely and cost effective. When resources are limited—as they are for most organizations these days—improvement and cost must be carefully balanced.

A comprehensive measurement system must produce information on trends for both the continuous improvers and the breakthroughers. But the speed with which the improvement needs to be implemented depends on the underlying strategic plan. Plans can be established with the simple idea of getting "better," but this sort of plan doesn't challenge anyone or provide for accountability. Organizations usually find it better to set specific goals so there is agreement on how much "better" will be considered success—for example,

○ To ship at least 92 percent of orders within three days of receipt,

○ To decrease average work-in-process inventory to $500,000 by the end of the year, or

○ To reduce the cost per average sales call to $150 by the end of the quarter.

As measures become an important part of the organization's culture, more alternatives on which to base goals become available. Goals are no longer limited to, say, 10 percent more. It is possible to judge the level of performance using data from different parts of the organization or even using data from other organizations. Such benchmarking projects with one or more external partners are becoming very popular for improved goal setting.

Most measurement approaches make the mistake of not linking trend and level information. The improvement rate is managed monthly or quarterly by middle managers operating in somewhat of a vacuum. The major goals are reviewed from time to time by senior managers but are not usually based on routinely available information. The extent to which goals compete or are even mutually exclusive is not well recognized. Periodic campaigns drive one lagging goal at the risk of disrupting the attainment of other goals. Thus, the *routine* integration of improvement trends with benchmarked levels and goals is required.

7. The family of measures must be consistent with rewards, recognition, and management style.

Many families of measures are tied to reward and recognition systems. Certain percentage improvements or attaining a specified level of points results in a commendation (an atta-boy or atta-girl), an award (such as a plaque, gift, or special dinner), or even additional money (as with gainsharing plans).

In a general sense, the criteria for the leading quality awards could be construed as families of measures. Applicants are judged against a finite set of criteria, the sections are weighted, and a total score determines a winner or loser. Some of the awards and certifications, such as ISO 9000, are actuallly measures of the capability of developing information rather than a judgment of actual results. The Malcolm Baldrige National Quality Award criteria stress the availability of data throughout the organization and actual performance results, with an emphasis on customer satisfaction. The Shingo Prize for Excellence in Manufacturing concentrates on actual results in productivity, quality, and customer satisfaction and is closest to representing a true family of measures.

Also behind a family of measures are some managerial style

considerations. The family of measures was created in the first place to make local operations more understandable to the workforce through feedback, open discussion, and voluntary corrective action. The choice of the measures and their weighting presents a public statement of current priorities that cannot be mistaken. A change in the measures is direct evidence of a change in strategy.

How to Create a Family of Measures

The impetus for creating a family of measures can come from three principal sources:

◊ *Top management.* Creating a comprehensive measurement system based on the family-of-measures approach requires top-level support. Since the approach emphasizes level-by-level inter-pretation of organizationwide strategic threads, an appropriate stra-tegic plan or equivalent must be in place. Frequently the first family of measures developed for an organization is designed for the top level and is used as a model to be emulated at lower levels in a cascading manner.

◊ *Middle Management.* In some cases, a midmanagement zealot sells the idea for a family of measures to top management with a promise to conduct some pilot projects in his or her area for later demonstration purposes when the measurement program is rolled out to the rest of the organization. There are some advantages to this pilot approach.

First, it is unusual to find full support for measurement at the top of an organization, in spite of CEO buy-in, and subtle resistance can wear down even the best of intentions. Also, measurement issues may be more difficult at the top, where strategic issues may be clear but only general in nature. It is much harder to declare corporate-wide improvement in customer satisfaction than to measure one type of satisfaction among one class of customers, which is what might be found at a lower level.

Moreover, some issues—such as ethical behavior, environmental concern, participative management, and international outlook—are difficult to examine on a broad scale. Although management will find artificial ways to measure those issues, only at the lower levels—where managers can chart the number of salespeople disciplined for lying, the number of pollution emissions violations, the number of people who remain on quality improvement teams for a significant amount of time, or the number of non-U.S. citizens among its supervisory ranks—can they comprehensively and accurately be tracked.

✿ *An outside firm.*　Occasionally the main impetus for measurement comes from pressure outside the organization. It is not unusual for key customers to require certain quality practices of their important suppliers. This applies more often to statistical process control than to general performance measures, but once a customer starts becoming active in checking progress of orders and cycle times, an alert supplier will want to track them to compile data on current problems and, more important, prevent future problems. Also, large supppliers may want their smaller distributors to track certain customer performance variables to complete the chain between that supplier and the end customer.

Regardless of where the family of measures originates, it is wise to involve representatives of those being measured in the development of the measures. Although a senior guru can undoubtedly make a good guess as to what the "folks" would come up with, such an approach lacks the vital buy-in from the measurees. And this buy-in is what makes the measures a source of positive creativity (which encourages staff to determine how they can develop ideas to improve the measures) rather than negative creativity (which leads them to invent ways to beat the measures).

Although a small committee of measure developers can surely come up with a measurement system, the best results occur when a representative group of workers uses brainstorming techniques, such as the nominal group technique (NGT), to create measures.

Building a Family of Measures

With NGT, eight to ten people concerned with the work of a department or business process meet to generate a list of potential measures in a way that eliminates premature criticism and intimidation. The measures are sorted, grouped, and evaluated, and the group members recommend a solution that they have arrived at by consensus to the relevant senior manager. (NGT is discussed in greater detail in Chapter 12.)

Many good measurement systems have been developed entirely internally. For example, a department head, supervisor, or other leader learns about measurement and then guides his or her staff through the process, which is then copied throughout the organization. Sometimes consultants have been used early in the process to ensure consistent training and application among a group of "missionaries," who then go out and implement the measurement program. In other cases, consultants have run demonstration NGT groups and trained internal representatives to conduct subsequent sessions. Consultants are also sometimes retained to issue silent critiques and coach the internal facilitators through the entire process.

Regardless of how a proposed family of measures is developed, it should be tested with real data—first backward (if possible) and then forward. If the measures selected are fairly ordinary measures already in existence, go back a year or two and put the actual historical data into the new format and see if it would have been helpful or have provided an insight missed the first time. For example, if sales to a class of customer are off significantly this year, examine the year's order-cycle time record and compare it against order-cycle times for previous years. Perhaps the sales downturn could have been prevented with prompt recognition of any order-cycle time problems uncovered by the comparison. If most of the measures are new original measures, this is not possible.

There should also be a break-in period for the organization to assess what kinds of interpretation problems might crop up. In an organization that communicates clearly and effectively, the family of measures can be instituted with the understanding that the results are to be viewed as tentative for the first few time periods until the organization is comfortable with the measurement process. If, however, the organization's culture promotes an "If it's on paper, then it's gospel" mentality, it would be wise not to splash early results all over the place. Here, feasibility testing would have to be conducted out of sight of the line managers.

Whether evolutionary or revolutionary, the ultimate launch of the measurement program needs to be accompanied by as much focused discussion as possible on the expected feedback practices, on the fact that management is not looking to blame any individual or group for any problems that the measurement system reveals, and on the central continuous improvement motive that drove the creation of the family of measures in the first place.

☼ **3** ☼

Families of Measures in Action

When we hear the term "big picture," we tend to envision a company CEO or an important government official looking beyond the competing and often contradictory details on the reams of paper cluttering his or her desk to focus on what the organization's key stakeholders truly want. That individual's focus is reduced to the one measure that everyone agrees is important, if not most important—the bottom line. In the private sector, that measure is usually earnings per share; in the public sector, a cost versus budget number.

In our mind's eye, we can see that person stating as Roger Smith, former head of General Motors, once said, "I look at the bottom line. It tells me what to do."[1] The problem is, that kind of automatic-pilot mentality almost sank GM—and many other firms. "What to do" should always be a subtle combination of satisfying current customers, looking at the long-term product and service mix and employee revitalization, and, yes, even controlling costs.

Fortunately, the best leaders now realize that Smith and many others like him had too narrow a focus. Concentrating on immediate expenses and revenues shifts an organization's focus away from the equally vital outcomes expected by customers and the long term need for a vibrant workplace and community. So the big picture is actually painted by using a family of four to six measures. At the upper echelons of an organization—the macro level—these measures reflect the balance between different stakeholder orientations and different time frames.

But this also holds true at the various lower levels. Instead of stockholders there are top executives, instead of nations there are states or cities, instead of thousands of employees there are hundreds, but a variety of complex issues must still be addressed. Even a small work group handling one production line in a plant has multiple stakeholders to consider and more data than it "needs." The group must balance the need for more production with the need for experimentation to find better methods and the need for more training hours and the need for machine maintenance time and the need to clean the place for tomorrow's tour group. Yes, the group members also need a big picture—big for them, if not for the CEO. The family of measures provides a focus to return to whenever too much data are around. The key is to have a family of measures established not only at the macro level but at every critical level in the organization.

At medium levels, such as division or department levels and in cross-cutting business processes, there would be separate but related families of measures. For example, one person in the credit department might be the department's delegate to the customer complaint handling team, which also includes people from sales, production, and engineering. The customer-complaint-handling process should have its own family of measures, even if that process doesn't have a formal leader and doesn't occupy its own neat little box on the organizational chart.

At the micro level, every person is directly covered by at least one family of measures that gauges his or her immediate work group or production section. These individuals would also be indirect participants at each higher level—their department, division, plant, and company—but they would personally receive feedback only at the work group level.

Key Differences Between Families of Measures

Having families of measures everywhere in the organization doesn't mean that they all are the same. Even though they reflect common strategic threads from the top of the organization as much as possible, they are composed of different specific measures that pertain to local work requirements—that is, the work requirements of a particular unit, division, department, or group. Measures at the top of the organization and measures nearer the bottom typically differ in nature, frequency of measurements, source, and controllability.

Nature

At the top of the organization, many of the measures will be aggregated financial measures, such as profit level, multilocation cost ratios or quality costs, new product billings or ratios, and investment profiles. Nearer the bottom of the organization, where activities center on the physical production of a product or the delivery of a service, the measures will also tend to be physical, such as yield, scrap, labor productivity, energy use, order times, shipping deadlines made, and specific market penetration. Smart managers use the information they gather from lower-level measures to help refine goals made at the upper levels, but without going overboard. For example, Fred Fetterolf, former president of Alcoa, once noted that his company's operating plans "were developed in a new way, with the primary emphasis on a long list of nonfinancial measures of performance, such as safety, delivery, scrap rates, machine uptime, and inventory reduction. By paying attention to these things which we can control, financial success follows. We now have a great deal of information available to us that we never had before, and a new management challenge for some of us is to be careful not to use the information to micromanage the company."[2]

Frequency of Measurement

A family of direct operating measures for a group of production workers may have all or most of its physical data available daily, with a weekly focus meeting or work area display. For an entire plant or major service unit, the feedback and correction cycle is normally monthly. For more exotic support groups and groups nearer the top of the organization, much of the data becomes somewhat subjective or indirect and may be gathered from customers by survey methods. Here quarterly measurement is often sufficient.

Source

Physical data can often be directly and routinely gathered from logs, shipping reports, releases, or machine counters. Cost data come from accounting systems, which sometimes have problems with timeliness and allocation practices and philosophy. Customer data can be collected routinely or via special survey by the customer, the company itself, or a third party. The critical factor for all trend data is consistency. If the data are gathered the same way at the same point each time, many of the small criticisms regarding accuracy can be ignored.

Some data may be surrogate data—that is, measurement of a related variable rather than of the target variable. For example, pure creativity is difficult to measure, but numbers of original designs or variations, ideas generated, changes made, or awards received are all potentially correlated with creativity and can be assessed.

Controllability

Families of measures at the micro level often represent things or activities that are directly handled by the measurees. The family results clearly show any tradeoff decisions made by the team. The team members may not have policy control, but once policy is set, they are fully empowered to execute it. In contrast, the families at the macro level reflect policy directions that senior executives can certainly influence, but simply declaring a policy direction doesn't mean that the organization will automatically shift course.

A Family of Measures at the Macro Level

At the top of a company or government agency, "big picture" measures deal with the whole organization, change relatively slowly, and are sometimes hard to quantify precisely. Table 3.1 shows an example of a family of measures that might be found at the top of a manufacturing organization.

In this case, the strategic plan called for continued improvement in the base business—represented by value added per employee and market share—and special attention to three topics: WIP, new products, and environment. The two base measures make up 50 percent of the weight and have historically been recorded and seen improvement. The WIP measure tells the manufacturer, which is striving for flexible and lean production, just how well it is meeting its goals of customer-driven customization of products and service and quick changeover from one product to another. Structured as a percentage of the sales of all products, the sales of new products measure provides the manufacturer with data that reflect both the

TABLE 3.1. AN EXAMPLE OF TOP-LEVEL MEASURES

Measure	Weight
Value added per employee	25%
Market share of products A–D	25
Value added per work-in-process (WIP) inventory	20
Sales of new products developed over the last three years versus sales of all products	20
Environmental index	10
Total	100%

THE POWER OF PERFORMANCE MEASUREMENT

success of new product research and development and the success of those products in the field. The environmental index measure—which covers key emission levels, the amount of hazardous waste hauled off, and recycling rates—reflects the manufacturer's concern with various environmental issues and constraints.

It is interesting to note, however, which measures are *not* included in this company's family of measures: process quality, safety, and cycle time. This firm chose to track those indicators at the plant or region level. Naturally, improvements in quality and cycle time will lead to improvements in value added per employee, WIP, and ultimately market share.

Another important indicator—customer satisfaction—is reflected in the manufacturer's current market share measure, but after the fact. In a company with relatively few products, senior managers may want to include customer satisfaction data obtained through survey data in its family of measures. But in this complex organization, customer survey information will be emphasized at the plant and division levels because the organization has a wide variety of customers and it would be difficult to interpret the array of customer issues from the top without stepping on division managers' toes.

The data for three of this manufacturer's five measures would come directly from financial records. It's possible that some of the cost-related components of the environmental index could also be tracked through financial documents. Only market share and some of the other environmental components, such as emissions levels, would be physical data.

The top management group would review the results of the family every quarter and issue any necessary pronouncements accordingly. But some members of top management would analyze some of the components more often in their roles as department or division heads. The marketing director would possibly review market-share data every week. The operations manager and the lawyers might look at components of the environmental index every week. But in its policy-making stance, the executive group as a whole would formally review the family of measures on a quarterly basis.

A Family of Measures at the Middle Level

In the middle of an organization, the issues being measured are still recognizably related to those at the top, but they are restricted to specific product lines, processes, plants and regions, or cost categories. Many of these measures are easy to understand, but there are still some difficult categories, such as innovation, ethics, and community relations, that require indirect measurement. Table 3.2 shows an example of a family of measures from an insurance company's regional claims office.

TABLE 3.2. AN EXAMPLE OF MIDDLE-LEVEL MEASURES

Measure	Weight
Customer satisfaction survey results	30%
Total settlement cost per claim	25
Claims-processing cycle time	20
Documentation index	15
Sales leads	10
Total	100%

After a claim is settled, each claimant receives a survey form with which to rate the claims office on several aspects of its work. The return rate for these surveys is high, but many of the respondents are inherently unhappy. There are two ways to make claimants a lot happier: (1) give them more money than they are legitimately entitled to and (2) settle very rapidly. Since these are high-cost alternatives, this regional claims office must strike a balance between ensuring customer satisfaction and preserving the rights of the insurer. Thus, the three elements that affect that balance—customer satisfaction, settlement cost, and cycle time—must be measured. Added to the mix are two of the regional managers' pet projects: improving promptness and accuracy of documentation and helping salespeople obtain additional sales leads by being alert to customers' comments and complaints as their claims are being processed.

In this example, only the settlement cost data are derived from the office's financial accounting system. The rest of the data are physical. The cycle-time and documentation-completion-time data are recorded in log form as part of the office workers' computerized paperwork. Documentation accuracy is assessed through spot checks. The salespeople provide sales-lead data through a form of thank-you note that they send to claims processors when they have received a lead.

The regional office reviews the family of measures data every month, although various managers within that office might examine individual family members more frequently.

A Family of Measures at the Micro Level

Work groups in the factory and office also need families of measures for guidance. These measures are usually quite simple and direct but they can shift very quickly, requiring frequent measurement and analysis. Table 3.3 shows an example of a family of measures for a production team on the factory floor.

The standard production trilogy—units per hour, defects, and on-time delivery—is here, taking up 70 percent of the attention. But there is also a measure for team member cross-training and safety. When there is a variety in the units being produced, as there is in this scenario, it's important to use weighted units so that the first measure isn't unduly influenced by uncontrollable shifts in the

TABLE 3.3. AN EXAMPLE OF MICRO-LEVEL MEASURES

Measure	Weight
Weighted units produced per employee hour	25%
Defect rate	25
On-time delivery	20
Certifications per employee	20
Safety (OSHA reportables per period)	10
Total	100%

product or service mix. As in the claims office, three important things are being balanced on a day-to-day basis here. But as the last two measures show, attention is also given to the long-term development of employee capabilities.

The measures are entirely physical. The data are gathered on the floor, automatically (unit count and defect rate) and manually (hours, delivery times, safety, certification progress).

Some of the individual family members are measured as often as by the minute and discussed by the appropriate team every day. The aggregated family is discussed weekly and becomes a part, albeit a small part, of the operations manager's plantwide monthly report. Unlike at the macro and middle levels, here corrective action is assumed to have already been taken by the time any reports are compiled. There is no time for discussion through channels if the defect rate suddenly goes up or if deliveries are not made. Predetermined troubleshooting occurs among and between the production teams until the problem is uncovered. Only in the rare instance when the solution time is extended does the problem become part of the middle- and macro-level databases.

Testing a Family of Measures

Whether you already have families of measures in place or are ready to launch a newly created family of measures, it is important to set up a testing or critique mechanism to avoid the errors commonly made in developing such families. Here are six questions to ask yourself to help assess the effectiveness and thoroughness of your families of measures.

1. Are we leaving out something significant?

If the measures mechanically fit the official strategic plan elements that have been passed down, then the test is something of a test of the official strategic plan. Typically, local managers incorporate some pet issues that don't appear to contradict the official strategic threads into the list of measures. For example, there may be some interest in measuring absenteeism in the field. Although most modern organizations wouldn't consider this one of the top five issues— except perhaps in special situations, such as airplane crew scheduling and telephone hotline reception—it could certainly be incorporated into a family of measures. The only harm in doing so would be if absenteeism, or another low-priority concern, bumps customer order time or another important item, which might be initially harder to measure, from the list.

Concepts that may be contained in the strategic plan but that are not easily measured are also commonly omitted. An advertising agency, for example, can measure billings, renewals, and market share, but if it doesn't try to measure creativity, it won't get a complete picture of its performance and of what's required to ensure success. The measure may well be taken in an indirect fashion—through outside surveys or evaluations, for example—or reflect some sort of surrogate data—such as different ideas submitted or awards received—but it should be there.

The U.S. Department of Defense, for example, has an overriding "preparedness" objective that is difficult to measure directly. But when phrased in terms of the response of a particular command, base, or unit in a specific situation, that objective boils down to cycle times and units of people and equipment that can fairly easily be measured.

2. Are the measures inconsistent with individual motivations?

Since you do, indeed, get what you measure, it is critical to coordinate group and individual measures. Periodic individual appraisals and reviews are rarely well conducted by any organization. The issues that they address often reflect antiquated formal specifications that are of little current value. If secretaries are now administrative associates who are portrayed as key players on improvement teams and project units, their individual appraisal sessions should concentrate on feedback concerning teaming skills, project outcomes, and overall personal development rather than shorthand speed and appropriateness of dress. If machine operators or maintenance technicians are now immersed in the world of computer-based diagnostics or control, their evaluation should not continue to be based on length of service, absenteeism, and knowledge of hand tools.

No matter how dominant the team ethic has become, it is still individuals who get up in the morning, show up for work, and give their team the next new idea or leadership nudge. As Robert Persig wrote in *Zen and the Art of Motorcycle Maintenance*, "Any further improvement of the world will be done by individuals making Quality decisions. . . . We've had that individual Quality in the past, exploited it as a natural resource without knowing it, and now it's just about depleted."[3] Therefore, organizations shouldn't continue insulting key individuals by evaluating their performance with obsolete and mechanical formats.

3. Are the proper authority, tools, and training available to ensure accurate measurement?

The elements of the family of measures at each level should be reasonably controllable by the people at that level. Total control is rare. But if the basic concept of a product or service is faulty, no amount of teamwork or individual effectiveness will save the day. When you measure a poorly designed process, you're sure to obtain poor results.

For example, it is outrageous for a faceless telemarketing manager somewhere to think that a consumer might buy something over the phone at dinner time. The telephone marketers assigned to that hour should call another time zone, if they have the authority to do so, or rebel, for the basic service design doesn't allow them to succeed.

Sometimes an outsider can more easily assess whether additional authority, tools, or training are needed. In one factory where operators run several side-by-side machines, measurement revealed slow processing and flawed products. After the machines had been running a while, small leaks dripped to the floor. As the operators went from machine to machine, they sidestepped the puddles that accumulated. But they never noticed the additional step they were taking until it was pointed out to them by an observer from another line. Once drip pans were installed, the results went back to normal. Subsequently, all the machine operators were trained in total productive maintenance and completed a project whereby the machines were taken apart and sealed, which eliminated other minor problems that collectively had been robbing the line of both quantity and quality.

4. Can the measures be updated as needed?

Are the members of the family of measures reviewed, say, each year to see if they still reflect the current strategic interests of the current management, given the current state of staffing and capability? For long-standing families, how much change or adjustment has actually occurred in the measures?

As described here, families of measures meet many of the characteristics of what Margaret Wheatley, borrowing from quantum physics, calls "dissipative structures" in her book *Leadership and the New Science*.[4] She describes a situation where "the system let go of its present form so that it could reemerge in a form better suited to the demands of the present environment . . . [and] open systems maintain a state of non-equilibrium, keeping the system off-balance so that it can change and grow."

A well-designed family of measures strikes a balance among several measures while maintaining a creative tension among them because many times a choice is forced or a tradeoff is made between two elements, such as quality and cost or timeliness and documentation. When the tension dissipates, it may be because the organization has learned to cope with this particular set of measures. It is then time to incorporate some new ones into the family to stimulate the growth of the unit being measured.

Families of Measures in Action

5. Are the measures consistent with group rewards and recognition?

Is there consistency between reward systems and the actions implied by the local measurement system? Gainsharing systems that measure only labor productivity have survived into the modern age, even though labor costs are a small part of the overall costs for many businesses. Some team-based organizations have team-of-the-month-type competitions that focus on trivial internal team processes rather than on team outcomes as reflected in a family of measures.

In profit-sharing and ESOP environments, employees will sometimes take on what they perceive to be CEO-type behavior and embark on cost-saving or speed-up actions that are actually counterproductive. Lacking a clear local family of measures, they create their own, often to the detriment of the work process and overall efficiency. Even in an empowerment situation, supervision and mentoring are critical. Ideally, the group incentive plan is designed and communicated in a way that provides a strong and direct indication of the "things we need to do," such as reduce cycle time, meet customer delivery schedules, and eliminate specific kinds of waste. With such a plan, managers, supervisors, and employees are all working off the same signals and automatically integrate their efforts.

6. Do the measures foster good customer and supplier relations?

Does the family of measures make sense to internal and external customers and to the suppliers of the group in question? Ideally, the customers and suppliers were involved in creating the measures. But have the measures evolved through frequent contact with those interest groups?

Well-meaning individuals who assume they know what customers and suppliers want can be dangerous. For example, common sense management suggests that if late deliveries are a problem, the solution would be to have deliveries arrive as early as possible. To some customers, however, early deliveries are as bad as late deliveries. There is a specific window of opportunity to hit. Similarly, dock hands who take it on themselves to "improve" a truck-loading pattern may actually enrage a customer whose firm has locked the old pattern into its unloading procedure.

The way to avoid these situations is through meaningful two-way communication. It is impossible to spend too much time talking to customers and suppliers about what you are trying to do and how you measure what you are doing. Only they can tell you whether any current or proposed schemes work for them, and they are the reason you are in business.

If a family of measures can pass these six tests, it is well on its way to being a useful improvement tool for the group that owns it. It will become the consistent central frame of reference for everyone in the organizational unit, thus substantially reducing the amount of traditional "supervision" needed to keep the work processes flowing. Progress (or lack of progress) on the measures will drive directed and voluntary corrective action or the rebalancing of schedules and resources to meet customers' requirements.

SECTION II

✺

Beyond the Bottom Line

The search for the bottom line dominates business analysis. For private-sector businesses the level and trend of earnings per share are paramount, with maybe a little attention devoted to return on equity, return on capital, return on investment, and return on sales thrown in for good measure. In the public sector there are equivalent budget-conformance bottom lines. Yet these bottom lines, which may play a useful role in business communication, are of virtually no value in understanding how a business is operating. Trying to assess an organization's health simply by looking at its bottom line can lead to all manner of distortions, both intentional and accidental. Meaningful diagnosis requires a substantial breakdown of the bottom line into many "midsection lines" throughout the business.

Two of the main factors to consider in looking beyond the bottom line are productivity and profitability. These indicators are closely related, especially near the top of the organization. The major but vital difference is that productivity measures remove the distorting effects of inflation. Toward the bottom of the organization, the term *productivity* tends to conjure threatening images. Head count, as calculated to determine labor productivity, gets confused with head cut, as in downsizing. But when productivity analysis is extended to include a simultaneous examination of materials, energy, capital, information cost, and other key variables, a different and more comprehensive view of organizational health usually emerges.

Cost is a cousin of both profitability and productivity and plays a key role in calculating both. To use cost data properly, organizations must acquire an understanding of both weighting systems and price deflation. They also must factor in the importance of time, which is possibly more fundamental than any of the other measures. Time is a commodity that everyone wishes they had more of, and it's timeliness that most customers demand, often before competitive pricing and top-notch quality.

Organizations committed to throughly analyzing the effectiveness of their processes soon discover that bottom-line profitability figures are meaningless without a fairly extensive search through the productivity and cost data that are their building blocks.

☼ 4 ☼

Profitability: Measures of the Financial World

The most common measure of performance for a corporation is the so-called bottom line—net after-tax profit. But to most observers, that number by itself says little. To be meaningful, it has to be compared to something else.

For example, you could start by comparing this year's net after-tax earnings—say, of $2,876,543—with last year's $2,345,678—an improvement of 22.6 percent. If either or both years' figures were affected by a special occurrence, however, the amount must be recomputed accordingly. For example, if the corporation had a writeoff of $200,000 last year, then the adjusted base for last year is $2,545,678, which means that the corporation's improvement rate is only 13 percent. But cash flow is often a more accurate measure of corporate health than after-tax income. Cash flow includes income as well as noncash charges, such as depreciation, that represent monies just as available as profit dollars for accomplishing corporate objectives.

For most purposes, however, it is better to look at profitability on a before-tax basis. Tax rates are set by the government, and most changes in the effective tax rate are out of management's control. In the rare instance when the tax rate is affected by management savvy—for example, by switching forms of investing excess cash or by moving a plant outside the country—observers are still mostly interested in the underlying health of the organization as reflected in before-tax numbers.

If those at the top of the organization are interested in the ultimate bottom line, it follows that as you go lower in the organization, you go up the income statement, excluding uncontrollables. Just above before-tax income may be some earnings from unconsolidated subsidiaries or special investments, which are relevant to only that subsidiary or special group. Then there is corporate overhead. Some of that may be allocated to divisions, but when analyzing the major divisions or product lines that make up an organization, corporate overhead should be excluded to the extent that it pertains to corporate-level activity. Thus is invented an interesting hybrid—*contribution to overhead and profit.* Awkward as this term may sound, it is generally the best expression of profitability for a major division or product line because it leaves out major expense items that are not controlled at the division or product-line level.

When individual plants or regions are measured, yet another step may be taken up the income statement. In some cases, these operations essentially do not have control over their capital configuration. Their profitability can be measured only on a variable contribution or operating income that excludes all plant fixed costs or at least those associated with capital.

The last stop on the trip up the income statement is at or near the very top: sales or sales netback, which is sales less all variable sales and marketing costs. This represents the outcome of the sales effort. One variation in volatile organizations is "same store" sales, which excludes sales data from stores that were not operating during both periods of the comparison.

A Variety of Denominators
for Calculating Return

So far, profitability has been expressed only by a trend in absolute numbers of profit equivalent at various organizational levels. But this measure does not reveal the *adequacy* of the level of profits. A large trend improvement that rapidly takes the corporation from "horrible" to "fair" performance still leaves us with an underachieving organization. To chart adequacy, it is helpful to create profitability ratios where the level of profits is divided by various denominators related to the use of capital.

Long-Term Capital Employed

The most common and most useful denominator of return calculations is long-term capital employed. This comes unadjusted right off the balance sheet and is the sum of all long-term capital, regardless of source. A return used in return-on-capital (ROC) calculations includes profit and after-tax interest expense pertaining to long-term capital employed.

Although ROC is fundamentally important to the organization, its use can be highly misleading. In fact, its users are accustomed to making mental adjustments to compensate for any discrepancies. Money is money, after all, goes the reasoning. Who cares whether it's invested in food manufacturing, electronics, or retailing? It either earns more return or it doesn't. The problem, however, is the age (or vintage) and the nature of the underlying assets. The U.S. accounting system computes assets from historical cost without any adjustment for inflation or obsolescence. Thus, $1 million on a corporate balance sheet might be

○ A food canning plant built in 1954 for $3 million and two-thirds depreciated (some new equipment has been added, but the basic technology has changed little over time; estimated relacement value in 1994 is $10 million);

○ A pilot plant built by the same food company for $1 million in 1994;

○ A customized electronics plant built in 1989 for $1.3 million and designed to make 50 percent of the U.S. market for zigwats (because Korea turned out to be better at zigwat manufacture, this U.S. plant is operating at only 20 percent of capacity and is searching for other compatible products to make in the plant, even though zigwats emit impulses that interfere with other forms of chemical coating);

○ A retailing company that leases its buildings (the assets are almost entirely seasonal merchandise based on the "open" look; unfortunately, this turned out to be the year of the "closed" look, so the retailing company is closing out its open-look merchandise in South America at 80 percent off).

Folk accounting would say that only the pilot plant is "worth" $1 million right now. The variation outlined above is found across industries, within industries, and even within major companies, so it is difficult to be sure that someone's 16 percent ROC is truly better than someone else's 13 percent ROC. Within a company, the data from the various divisions can be adjusted or footnoted to explain the differences, but doing so is time-consuming and can lead to disagreements.

Here's an example of how accounting for capital can lead to incorrect conclusions. In the 1970s one food industry conglomerate held an annual ROC sweepstakes where the division heads showed up at headquarters for judging. The perpetual winner, housed in a quonset hut, was the smallest division, which always had more than a 40 percent ROC because of its extraordinarily small capital base. After years of glory, the division finally built itself a real building. Not surprisingly, that ended the victory string and the division was spun off to management, which quickly found other lines to fill the new

Profitability: Measures of the Financial World

building. Thanks to this and other similar strategic mistakes, the conglomerate eventually went out of business.

Even within a small company or division, the ROC trend can be misleading. Table 4.1 shows how a decline in profitability can be explained using replacement cost accounting. The United States had a brief fling with replacement cost accounting in the mid–1980s to bring the nation "up" to the accounting level of much of the rest of the world. But the practice was abandoned as memories of the high inflation rates of the late 1970s faded, and the embarrassment that the new accounting methods would cause to many old-line companies became apparent. For even in good years major companies were showing negative earnings when assets and depreciation were rebased on replacement or reproduction cost.

Equity

Return on equity (ROE) is often used instead of ROC to gauge an organization's success. Unlike ROC, ROE does differentiate between debt and equity. In calculating ROC, the profit is divided only by

TABLE 4.1. OLD TYME JELLY, INC. SELECTED STATISTICS
(all amounts are in thousands of dollars)

	1993	1994
Sales	$5,000	$5,500
After-tax income	$ 300	$ 360
Assets employed:		
Inventory	$ 300	$ 330
Basic factory[a]	$ 500	$ 470
New equipment[b]	—	$ 700
Total assets	$ 800	$1,500
Income/assets employed	37.5%	24.0%
Income/assets employed		
(replacement cost)	5.7%	6.0%

[a] Cost $2 million to build in 1954; on the books for $500,000 in 1993; replacement cost is $5 million in 1994.
[b] Small addition increased capacity 10 percent; costs $700,000 in 1994.

equity, with the interest on long-range borrowed capital treated like any other expense. In a successful organization, this introduction of leverage can lead to more impressive results. And in a relatively stable business where maintaining debt is a normal and safe practice, ROE is a better reflection of management's business decisions than ROC is. But ROE is also often used where the debt adds much additional risk to the well-being of the company. Trying to compare company ROEs can be as difficult as comparing ROCs, with the added burden of variability between companies in amount and type of debt incurred.

ROE calculations are essentially useless below the level of the whole corporation because it's hard to trace ROE against the purpose for which the money is being borrowed. Free-standing divisions can identify their own building and equipment debt, but the leverage policy—that is, the debt-to-equity tolerance— of the organization as a whole is usually decided at the top and should not be debited or credited to subordinate operating managers. It's normal to use an ROC basis within a large organization that doesn't want its operating managers to worry about whether investments can be leveraged.

Complicating matters is the fact that the phrase *return on investment* (ROI) is frequently tossed around organizations, sometimes to mean either ROC or ROE. Most commonly, however, it is a capital budgeting measure used to sort out specific investment opportunities. The incremental operating cash flow expected from each candidate investment is laid out along with investments required, and the resulting net cash flow is discounted back to the current time frame using various investor interest rates. The investor interest rate that makes the investments and the future cash flows from those investments balance is the project's ROI. In the most mechanical conglomerates, the highest ROIs are funded until the available monies run out. More typically, if the calculation of ROI doesn't meet key executive expectations, the cash flows are "reestimated" until they do.

Profitability: Measures of the Financial World

Sales

Not all profitability ratios deal with capital. Return on sales (ROS) or gross margin on sales can give useful information about the organization on both a level basis and a trend basis. Assessing the "return" in return on sales is difficult in that it reflects many things that have little to do with the selling process. It is hard to compare ROS, even within an industry, because of the differences in what "return" means, not to mention differences in mix of product between companies and over time. But the differences are within the range of being correctable. ROS in the supermarket industry, for example, might require adjustment for the foods to nonfoods ratio, but with a clear-cut definition of what is and what isn't considered in "return" some insight can be obtained from a comparison. At least here there is nothing as complex as the asset vintage problem that often plagues calculations based on capital.

Gross margin is sales less variable costs associated with producing and marketing the product or service, compared to sales itself. There is sometimes difficulty defining what is variable. Some advertising campaigns, for example, have a fixed cost and some variable extensions. Within one organization, where infrastructure is not changing too rapidly, gross margin trend is useful. But across companies and across industries, there will be wide differences in how much capital is required to support the operations, and that is not reflected in the gross margin.

In interpreting ROS or gross margin, it is critical to understand the price effects that are included in the numbers. We are accustomed to thinking of inflation as being an overall economic concept. Therefore, if there is inflation in both the numerator and denominator of a ratio, it cancels out. But actually each product and service has its own price trend. A "market basket" of products and services is analyzed to come up with overall inflation indices, but, in fact, there is a separate inflation rate for potatoes, tomatoes, spices, canned items, carton goods, and so on.

Gross margin can improve because costs were reduced, or it can improve because the price of a product or service went up faster

TABLE 4.2. ACME YOGURT MANUFACTURING COMPANY
PROFITABILITY RATIOS
(all amounts are in thousands of dollars)

Income Statement

		PRODUCT LINES	
		A	B
Sales	$24,400	$10,000	$14,400
Less returns and discounts	(400)	(200)	(200)
Net sales	$24,000	9,800	14,200
Variable costs	(17,100)	(8,100)	(9,000)
Variable Contribution	6,900	1,700	5,200
Local overheads	(900)	(300)	(600)
Contribution to overhead and profit	6,000	1,400	4,600
Depreciation	(500)		
Interest on long-term debt	(200)		
Other overhead	(2,100)		
Earnings from unconsolidated subsidiary	200		
Net before-tax income	3,400		
Income tax	(1,400)		
Net after-tax income	2,000		

Balance Sheet

		PRODUCT LINES	
		A	B
Current assets	$10,000	$2,000	$8,000
Fixed assets	8,000	4,000	4,000
Total assets	$18,000	$6,000	$12,000
Current liabilities	$ 8,000		
Long-term debt	3,000		
Stockholders' equity	7,000		
Total liabilities	$18,000		

TABLE 4.2. ACME YOGURT MANUFACTURING COMPANY
PROFITABILITY RATIOS (*continued*)

Useful Profitability Ratios

Return on capital	After-tax income + Interest/equity + debt	21.0%
Return on equity	After-tax income/Equity	28.8%
Cash flow to equity	After-tax income + Depreciation/Equity	35.7%
Return on net sales	After-tax income/Net sales	8.3%
Gross margin	Variable contribution/Net sales	28.7%
Product line A		
Return on assets	Contribution to overhead + profit/	
	Assets employed	23.3%
Product line B		
Return on assets	Contribution to overhead + profit/	
	Assets employed	38.3%

than the "price" of the various labor and materials costs. Both are legitimate improvements in that they bring additional short-term monies into the business, but they are strategically quite different and involve different people in the organization. Table 4.2 demonstrates several profitability ratios at the fictional Acme Yogurt Manufacturing Company. For the whole company, return on capital, return on equity, cash flow to equity, and return on net sales are meaningful. For the two major divisions, gross margin for product lines A and B and contribution to overhead and profit over assets employed are used.

The Relationship Between Profitability and Productivity

An improvement in return on sales, subject to the conditions discussed above, reflects an improvement in profitability. But it is useful to separate "doing things better internally," such as cost reduction, from "doing things better in the marketplace," such as

TABLE 4.3. PROFITABILITY AND PRODUCTIVITY

Revenue	Value	=	Quantity	×	Price
	$ Steel sold	=	Tons of steel	×	Price per ton
	↓		↓		↓
	Profitability		*Productivity*		*Price Recovery*
	↑		↑		↑
Expenses	$ Payroll	=	Number of employees	×	Price (wage) per employee
	$ Steel	=	Tons of scrap	×	Price per ton of scrap
	$ Electricity	=	Kilowatt hours (KWH)	×	Price per KWH

aggressive pricing. Table 4.3 breaks down both sales and the constituent costs (two forms of value) into two components, quantity and price. It then demonstrates that if a revenue-to-expense ratio might be called profitability, there is a ratio of the underlying quantities that can be called *productivity* and a ratio of the underlying prices that can be called *price recovery.*

Thus, productivity can be thought of as profitability with the relative price effects removed, and price recovery can be thought of as profitability adjusted for quantities of input and output. Productivity is of great interest to the internal operations people, and price recovery is of great interest to sales and marketing and to purchasing—those who deal with the "outside world." Integrating the two is necessary in practice: that's what managers are for. But the first step to effective integration is understanding the key differences between the two factors. (The separation of productivity from national income statistics is discussed in Appendix A. Two models that analytically break apart profitability and productivity are presented in Appendix B.) The critical point to keep in mind is that profitability is not a valid workforce performance indicator, for there is no correlation between profitability level (such as ROC) and labor productivity (such as sales per employee) even in relatively stable industries, such as electric utilities and food processing (see Figures 4.1 and 4.2).

Profitability: Measures of the Financial World

FIGURE 4.1. ELECTRIC UTILITY INDUSTRY (1992)

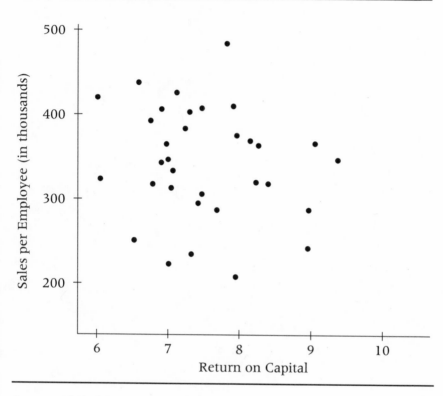

SOURCE: Value Line.

Profit on Wall Street

The most common profitability ratio used on Wall Street is growth in earnings per share (EPS). The earnings are net profit with appropriate comparability adjustments, such as nonrecurring expenses, reorganizations, or accounting practice changes. For companies without much seasonality or exposure to the business cycle, EPS trends are considered very clear indicators of progress, and even minute variations from expected levels lead to large stock price adjustments.

FIGURE 4.2. FOOD INDUSTRY (1992)

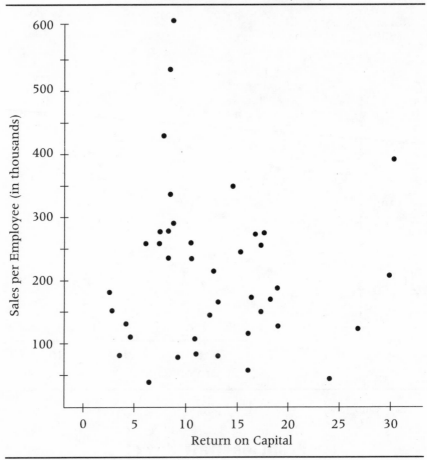

SOURCE: Value Line.

A ratio of price to earnings is the basic Wall Street value base. Experts carry mental benchmarks of the appropriate price to earnings (P/E) ratios for various types of stocks and industries. One general rule of thumb for growth companies is that the P/E ratio shouldn't be much higher than the expected EPS growth rate. But with the current wave of restructuring writeoffs and special adjustments, the P/E ratios have been higher than this rule normally allows. When a sudden earnings decline raises the P/E ratio above the mental benchmark, there is pressure to sell the stock until the price drops enough so that the appropriate correction can be made. Companies with business-cycle or commodity-price exposure often prefer to use cash flow per share as an even more basic measure of corporate health and ability to survive.

The Various Meanings of "Profit"

In the private sector, careless use of the word *profit* can be dangerous. When dealing with numerical data, approximately right is better than precisely wrong. When tracking numerical trends, consistency is the absolute requirement. Each component of the trend must be calculated in the same way.

At the top of the organization, return on capital employed and trend in earnings per share or cash flow per share are the most valuable measures. But return on equity and return on sales can be used in circumstances where the base of comparison is carefully chosen.

In the middle of the organization, controllability is key. The best solution here is a ratio with a numerator of either contribution to corporate overhead and profit or variable contribution (if local overheads are not controlled locally) to the unit's assets employed or to net sales.

Even when done perfectly, such calculations alone are not sufficient indicators of an organization's performance. Profit numbers provide good input to the strategic planning process, but they do not have much diagnosis or improvement value unless they are broken down into their physical constituents.

The most practical alternatives to profit in many public-sector organizations are budget variance for the short term and growth in budget compared to outcomes for the long term. Performance against budget is an understandable and comprehensive measure,

PROFIT IN THE PUBLIC SECTOR

It is easy to say that there is no equivalent of profit in the public sector or in not-for-profit organizations and be done with it. However, statements can be made about the overall performance of a public-sector organization, which, in some respects, takes the place of profits as the focal point of a public organization's strategic deliberations.

Where the public-sector organization has direct equivalents in the private sector, profit accounts can be created in the same manner as in the private sector. Public-owned utilities, transport systems, hospitals, and many others can be compared with private-sector counterparts up to the before-tax income line, as long as the "surplus" is not to be routinely rebated to suppliers or customers, as it is in a cooperative. Thus, rate of improvement in before-tax profit, conribution, or whatever it's called can be made and interpreted with some stretch.

A major problem is that many true public-sector organizations don't have a concept of "capital." Money previously spent was spent regardless of whether it had value beyond that accounting period. Thus, public-sector organizations in this situation can calculate a form of ROS, but not ROC and certainly not ROE. A return on assets employed could be created through original appraisal of apparent assets, but this would be time consuming and expensive to repeat every year if the accounting and appropriation systems are not changed at the same time.

but it has two nearly fatal weaknesses. When budget variance is the measure of performance, there's tremendous incentive for managers to play budgeteering games in the beginning and during the period in question to ensure appropriate cushions against shortfalls in later performance. Variance against budget is as much a measure of budgeting skill as it is of operating performance. The other problem is that insufficient attention is given to output and especiallly to outcome. Some budgeting techniques do adjust the variable component-to-output volume, but the fixed-variable break is often arbitrary, and rarely is shift in the difficulty of output mix or inflation in budgeted costs handled well, if it all.

Presumably, the public sector exists to do things (outcomes) that can't be done well or fairly by the private sector. Yet the measures of success don't directly incorporate the achievement of those outcomes—graduated students, literate students, lives saved, degree of military readiness, crimes solved or prevented, and so on. As of this writing, the United States federal government is emphasizing outcomes and has mandated the development of customer-based measures derived from explicit strategic plans and implemented by empowered workers with access to measured results.[1] Perhaps a later edition of this book can celebrate the full success of this initiative.

☼ 5 ☼

Productivity: Measures of the Physical World

The word *productivity* is often used as an umbrella term to cover all good things related to organizational improvement. It is often interchanged with *quality, excellence, growth, competitiveness, effectiveness, participative management,* and even *ethical behavior* and *fertility.* But it also has a narrower and more specific definition.

Productivity is the relationship between the outputs of a process and one or more inputs to that process. *Process* can mean any level of work involving an organization, ranging from a small part of what passes through one person's work station to a departmental task and on to a key process of the entire organization. If only one input is considered, the resulting ratio is called *partial.* If more than one input is used, the ratio is *multiple.* If all inputs are used, a *total* productivity ratio results. A wide variety of outputs and types and combinations of inputs make productivity analysis a surprisingly rich and useful measurement technique.

Measures of Output

At the top of the organization, productivity often borrows from profitability analysis and uses financial output measures, such as sales or value added—sales less purchased goods and services—for its more general ratios. But the basic intent of all productivity analysis is to reach the underlying physical operations and see if they are done well or are improving. Financial data can be helpful in productivity trend analysis, but only if they are expressed in "constant dollars" with inflationary effects removed.

A critical part of determining the output of a selected process is to carefully define the end point of the process. While the best measure of a whole organization's output is at the very end of the production process, where the product is turned over to the external customer, there are other intermediate points in a major process that are also of interest. In a plywood manufacturing plant, for example, at least thirteen different physical measures of output can be compared to appropriate parts of the labor-capital resource input:

- Logs prepared,

- Veneer peeled (thickness adjusted),

- Clippable surface,

- Green veneer weight,

- Drying surface (thickness and variety adjusted),

- Dry veneer weight,

- Prepared faces,

- Core plys,

- Panels,

- A or B faces,

Productivity: Measures of the Physical World

○ Panels' weight,

○ Special panels, and

○ Panels shipped (configuration adjusted).

Such a proliferation of measures is not limited to manufacturing. Most service-industry processes have several intermediate checkpoints before the last transaction with the final customer. In a typical hotel, for example, outputs may include.

○ Rooms rented,

○ Guests accommodated,

○ Checkout transactions,

○ Beds made,

○ Line items charged to room,

○ Phone calls handled,

○ Baggage manipulations,

○ Cars valet parked,

○ Reservations made,

○ Concierge inquiries handled,

○ Conventions hosted, and

○ Maintenance transactions completed.

And all this is before meal service is even considered!

The challenge is to match each output with the correct related input(s) to get a meaningful productivity ratio—that is, output divided by inputs. In a steel mill, for example, tons of steel produced per production worker makes an excellent labor productivity ratio. Tons of steel per production scheduler makes some sense because more (or fewer) schedulers may be needed to offset major increases (or decreases) in tonnage. (Batches of steel per scheduler is probably better, however.) Tons of steel per security guard makes no sense at all; here, the inputs and outputs relevant to a process (steelmaking) have been misaligned. The output of security guards, however, can be expressed in square feet protected, visitors handled, and the like.

Labor Productivity

By far the most common productivity ratio reflects labor productivity—output divided by related labor input. The labor input can be represented by either labor hours or number of employees. Using labor hours will result in a more accurate ratio, especially in a situation where there are substantial overtime hours or substantial part-time or temporary employees. But if hours are bundled as *employee equivalents*, it doesn't matter whether number of labor hours or number of employees is used to represent labor input. Number of employees is easier to calculate and explain than labor hours and is used where only an approximation is desired or where most of the employees are on salary, so that the number of hours worked cannot be easily calculated.

If the number of labor hours is used, those taking the measure must choose between using hours paid or hours at work. Financial ratios tend to use hours paid, which is easy to calculate and significant, since the company has, in fact, paid the workers regardless of whether they actually did any work. Hours at work is preferred for physical productivity ratios, which are designed to assess the basic health of the organization rather than what happened in a particular pay period. Even though employees may be absent for authorized reasons, absentees still are not doing work during their time away from the job. It would be even more accurate to use *hours working*, excluding idle and break times, but this is difficult to measure, and any attempt to do so would probably be interpreted by

Productivity: Measures of the Physical World

most workforces as a sign of excessive management control. Indeed, idle time often results from the scheduling system and not from employees' lack of drive.

Table 5.1 shows a simple labor productivity calculation in which the ouput (O) is divided by the labor input (L), which is the number of employees:

TABLE 5.1. A SIMPLE LABOR PRODUCTIVITY CALCULATION

	Last Year	This Year	Percent Change
Output (total number of megazogs)	100	120	20.0%
Labor input (number of employees)	40	44	10.0%
Labor productivity (O/L)	2.5	2.73	9.2%

It's important to note that despite the more than 9 percent increase in labor productivity, it is not necessarily true that these megazog workers performed "better" this year than they did last year. Perhaps an automatic megazog-making machine was installed, and, in fact, ten workers would have been sufficient in the current year. Any productivity ratio must be interpreted in its own context, ideally in reference to other partial ratios and maybe even a total productivity ratio to help interpret resource tradeoffs.

The financial counterpart of physical output is dollars of output (sales value) per dollar of payroll, with both output and input being expressed in constant dollars of the same year for trend analysis. In financial ratios, the labor input can be expressed as payroll or as payroll plus benefits. Inclusion of benefits is certainly needed in most statements of cost level, but they need to be included in trend calculations only if the percentage of benefits is changing over time. A constant benefit percentage added to successive payroll numbers doesn't affect the payroll change rate.

Caution needs to be exercised if some of what would normally show up as labor cost is occasionally converted into materials cost through subcontracting or if normally purchased subassemblies are suddenly brought in-house. For a trend comparison to be accurate and meaningful, all its elements must be consistent. Any exceptions need to be adjusted. Although the distinctions between direct and indirect labor are breaking down with factory-floor computers and self-managed teams, organizations sometimes wonder whether to include indirect employees in a productivity analysis. Again, the rule is consistency; make the same inclusions in all periods of the trend.

Another aspect of labor productivity to consider is whether the physical processes are, in fact, designed to run well. If employees are confronted with a system where the "official" way to do the work is awkward or inefficient, actual labor productivity will never reach an acceptable level, regardless of employee effort or diligence. To assess the effectiveness of a process, measures pertaining to it can be made: number of times the product needs to be handled, number of planned interruptions, number of reviews and inspections, number of transfers, and so on.

Materials Productivity

Most manufacturing companies develop measures to control the use of materials. A yield measure that compares the percentage of usable output to original materials input is essentially an upside-down materials productivity measure. Percentage of scrap, often separating "planned" and "unplanned" scrap, is another materials measure. Some cutting, molding, or punching processes have an unavoidable "standard" scrap that is tolerated to take advantage of less expensive gross raw material shapes.

In calculating materials productivity, care needs to be taken to specify at what point the raw material enters the process. Materials are first noted at the time of a purchasing transaction and again at the time of delivery. But a production manager may not officially assume control of the materials until they are put into the first production machine. On the other hand, some plant managers are also business managers responsible for purchasing raw materials. In this case, the material enters at the time of the purchase transaction or delivery.

To accurately match the output against the appropriate input base, the same kind of thinking has to take place at the end of the production process. The typical production manager may be finished with the product when it enters the product distribution warehouse, but the business manager may retain responsibility until the product is shipped or even until it's received by the external customer.

Bear in mind that there is always some chance of error in the physical counting procedures. Most materials-receiving operations consider both physical quantity and dollar value in their checking, but downstream from their actual receipt the physical count of those same materials can get careless. There is no disagreement on what constitutes a pound, linear foot, or ream, but problems can arise with terms like *piece* or *unit* unless careful definitions have been agreed on. When an organization sometimes receives a subassembly and sometimes receives the equivalent as three separate unassembled components, counting can get mixed up.

The concept of *case* also can be slippery. Some cases contain twenty-four 10-ounce cans and others may contain sixteen 13-ounce cans; simply counting gross cases can be misleading, unless there is a constant mix of type of case over time.

Finally, although the need to carefully control the use of major materials is obvious, what about the hundreds of minor materials? Should there be partial productivity ratios concerning sweeping compound, lubricants, and disposable coffee cups? The best practice is to lump together miscellaneous materials by major category (plastics, metals, wood or paper, chemicals) and occasionally run cost-per-output unit calculations, with the categorized costs being deflated by an appropriate deflator (for example, wood or paper by a forest products industry index).

Energy Productivity

Most organizations have little need to think about energy productivity. Energy is not a large percentage of their costs, and its control is quite visible and well accepted. But at manufacturing facilities where energy plays a key role in the process itself, energy productivity may be one of the main indicators of performance. In aluminum reduction and many chemical manufacturing processes, energy is the single largest cost.

In the simple case where there is one major form of energy, the energy productivity partial ratio is obvious: units of that energy used divided into some measure of product output. Where there are multiple forms of energy, and especially where there is a tradeoff between energy forms, an overall energy partial ratio is required.

A convenient way of expressing energy input is in British thermal units (BTUs). Every common form of energy has been rated as to its inherent BTU content, so we can simply add up the BTUs used and compare that number to product output. It may seem burdensome to constantly make such a calculation, but in the United States such calculations are required by law. The only trick in a large company is to locate the clerk who handles this obscure task.

For some more sophisticated purposes, the different forms of energy may be combined to take into account other factors besides BTU content. There are other, often substantial, costs associated with the basic use and even with the incremental use of each form of energy. Coal and heavy fuel oil are relatively inexpensive per BTU but generate significant costs in terms of storage and pollution control. Propane is expensive to store but clean burning. Natural gas can be inexpensive on an "interruptable" basis in some regions but may be quite expensive otherwise. If the BTUs are weighted by a full cost per BTU or an incremental cost per BTU, the resulting productivity trends may be quite different from results obtained via a simpler calculation.

Another problem with energy measurement is separating *produc-*

tion energy from *overhead energy.* Some energy costs are related to seasonal plant heating and cooling expenses, which are related to degree-days of weather but not to production level once the plant is operating. But the more significant energy costs are those associated with plant production volume, product type, or process chosen. The two can be separated by multiple regression techniques, but separate metering would make everyone's life much easier. Unfortunately, that is not always possible.

One frozen foods plant and warehouse complex that was a heavy user of electricity was stymied in its desire to analyze usage trends by production section by the local electric utility's unwillingness to permit installation of extra meters within one master billing account. Similar absurdities have occurred in situations where electric meters are a key basis of the local property tax assessment.

Yet another wrinkle must be considered when a plant starts "manufacturing" its own power with standby generators or forms of cogeneration. For example, forest products companies will sometimes burn sawdust and bark in their boilers (backing out normal fuel) and other times sell the sawdust and bark to outside customers. Keeping an accounting track of such practices is necessary to ensure an accurate overall measure of energy productivity.

Capital Productivity

Capital productivity is the relationship between a measure of output and a measure of capital input.[1] In productivity analysis, the dominant basis for capital input is assets employed, the so-called left side of the balance sheet. No one cares whether the assets were obtained through use of debt or retained earnings (right side), and usually no one cares whether the assets are classified as current or long-term. Some analysts will exclude seasonal working capital associated with raw material or finished goods buildups, but this starts a bad precedent of appeals for special treatment.

The timing of capital recognition is much like the question of when materials enter the process. Capital may enter the processes associated with a particular production manager only when the building or equipment represented is ready for use. But capital may enter much earlier for a project manager with control over construction or even site selection or land procurement.

Management must decide whether to express capital productivity in terms of nominal dollars or of replacement or replication cost. In dynamic situations with essentially nothing but new plants and equipment or in static situations where no change in the asset base has recently occurred or is being contemplated, there is no harm in using nominal dollar accounting. But where there is a mix of old and new assets and where additions (and deletions) are occurring every year, use of replacement or replication cost would be much less misleading. Unfortunately, most major organizations fall into the latter category.

Replication cost represents today's cost of building the old plants and equipment, calculated by applying appropriate producer price indices to the original purchase or construction costs, implicitly using the original technology. Replacement cost represents today's cost of building the equivalent capacity using today's technology.

For most purposes, replacement cost is a better measure to consider when determining capital productivity than replication cost. The cost of reproducing the 1947 Univac T–33 computer today, using equivalent vacuum tubes, would be billions of dollars. The cost of replacing its capacity is about $39.95 at Radio Shack. Replication cost is best applied to chemical and oil plants where each is a completely unique configuration that would be impossible to understand without using the original blueprints.

As long as the target of analysis is just capital productivity, the denominator can be some representation of assets employed from the balance sheet, adjusted or unadjusted. But for a multiple input ratio—say, labor *and* capital productivity or total productivity—the asset number would have to be annualized or adjusted to indicate what proportion of the assets apply to each year in question. This requires, in turn, an assumption about the suitable return rate for long-term invested money if these assets were instead invested in money markets.

The annual capital input for a multiple ratio is the sum of straight-line depreciation plus the "implicit" return mentioned above plus any leases employed. If assets employed have been put on a replacement or replication basis, then the amount of depreciation would be similarly adjusted automatically. Capitalized leases need to be converted to "equivalent" expense leases for the purpose of that calculation. The source of the assets employed isn't relevant; debt, retained earnings, and leasing are all the same. See Table 5.2 for a calculation of a multiple-input (labor and capital) productivity ratio for a base year.

Special attention must be paid to inventory ratios because of the current high interest in reduction of work-in-process inventory as part of the movement to lean, just-in-time production. A ratio of annual sales volume in dollars to current inventory in dollars is called *inventory turnover*. A higher number is good; it means more sales were supported by a specific level of inventory. This is also a

TABLE 5.2. A MULTIPLE- INPUT PRODUCTIVITY RATIO

Item	Calculation	Amount
1. Output of megazogs	—	$2,500,000
2. Employees	—	40
3. Average wage	—	$20,000
4. Payroll	2 × 3	$800,000
5. Assets employed	—	$2,000,000
6. Depreciation rate	—	6%
7. Depreciation expense	5 × 6	$120,000
8. Long-term money market rate	—	10%
9. Imputed return	5 × 8	$200,000
10. Expensed leases	—	$30,000
11. Capital input	7 + 9 + 10	$350,000
12. Labor and capital input	4 + 11	$1,150,000
13. Multiple input productivity	1 / 12	2.174

form of capital productivity ratio. In most manufacturing organizations, turnovers are calculated for total inventory, raw materials, work-in-process, and finished goods because each is driven by different policies and procedures.

Fixed-resource utilization is usually thought of as a capital productivity concept, but there is a subtle difference. A utilization ratio compares the time an asset is being "used" with the total time available for use. There is no assumption that the asset is being used efficiently when it is being used. Thus, a motorpool vehicle might be used 73 percent of the available time or 29 percent of the available time. The rate of use is of great interest when it's time to consider buying more vehicles or downsizing the fleet. But the relative efficiency of the use of the vehicles would be analyzed by something like person-miles carried by the vehicle. It might turn out that a vehicle with a 29 percent utilization rate is used infrequently but that when it is used, it carries four people hundreds of miles, thereby saving the organization airfare money. In contrast, a vehicle with a 73 percent utilization rate may do nothing but one-block mail runs that could just as well have been handled on foot with a pushcart.

The same kind of logic applies to other asset-utilization situations involving computer terminals, process machinery, factory and warehouse square and cubic footage, and corporate aircraft.

Other Partial Productivity Ratios

The breakdown of inputs into labor, materials, energy, and capital is clearly geared toward manufacturing processes. In the office and laboratory, however, other factors must be considered. For example, a *premises* partial ratio that includes floor space and furnishings (capital), utilities (energy), basic office and cleaning supplies (materials), and sanitation, security, and reception personnel (labor) may be useful. An *information* partial ratio that includes computer costs, library services, some consulting (not all consulting provides information), subscriptions, and perhaps courier services might also be useful.

In the factory, a *maintenance* partial ratio that includes both own and contracted maintenance labor, maintenance supplies and tools, and floor space and equipment for the maintenance shop is often created.

Total Productivity

Total productivity is the obvious next step beyond multiple productivity ratios. This includes *all* the inputs to a process compared to the output of the process. Purists—including the U.S. Bureau of Labor Statistics—will argue that it's impossible to come to a total measure because the underlying aspects of community development and well-being, human worth, ethics, and other abstractions cannot tangibly be assessed. Here we will use *total* to include all measurable inputs and leave it to others to quantify the rest.

Total productivity is the relation of output to all the (measurable) inputs, for example, the sum of labor, materials, energy, and capital (annualized). The closely related total factor productivity compares a value-added output—for example, sales less purchased materials and energy—to labor and capital annualized inputs. The same things are included in both calculations, but the trends will come out slightly differently.

The simplest way to calculate total productivity is to aggregate all the relevant partial productivity indices weighted by the relative importance of their input components, as shown in Table 5.3. If each partial ratio is fully inclusive of all costs in the category, the resulting calculation is accurate. However, the typical practice is to choose a representative partial input, especially in the materials and energy categories, which leads to an approximate productivity data total.

The simplest way to calculate total factor productivity is to use the same method as the one illustrated above, but of course there will

TABLE 5.3. TOTAL PRODUCTIVITY CALCULATION

	Input factor/ Weights (percent of input)	×	Partial productivity index	=	Weighted productivity improvement
Labor	30		1.050		.315
Materials	40		1.030		.412
Energy	10		.970		.097
Capital	20		1.010		.202
Total productivity					1.026

be only two lines of data—labor and capital. Materials and energy are considered purchased goods and services that are deducted from sales to determine the value-added output that will be divided by either labor and or capital.

An analytically richer approach to total productivity that applies best to a cost-center plant or business employs the idea of a set of frozen cost standards for each factor of production, including those generally thought of as fixed. Closely related to the concept of flexible budgeting, the approach starts with a matrix of the cost buildup of every product or service produced in a base year. It separates the unit cost of each ingredient from the standard recipe for the needed quantity of that ingredient. Variable ingredients, where the amount of input is directly related to the amount of output, generate a linear use function, as can be seen in Figure 5.1.

As Figure 5.2 shows, semifixed or fixed ingredients, such as floor space, where an amount of input covers a wide range of ouput levels (of fixed costs), generate a flat or stair-step use function.

Both the unit input costs and the recipe are then "frozen," and for future time periods a target for each input is established based on actual volume of output multiplied by the two frozen factors. Since the later-year targets will be in base-year dollars, the actual cost

Productivity: Measures of the Physical World

FIGURE 5.1. LINEAR USE FUNCTION

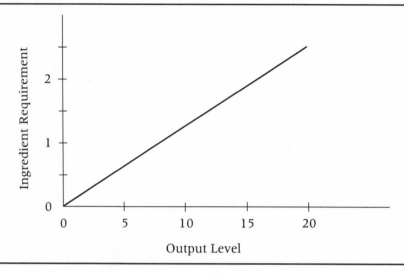

experience must be deflated back to base-year dollars to allow fair comparison with the targets. Each comparison of adjusted target recipe elements divided by the actual recipe used can be interpreted as a partial productivity ratio. A complete example is presented in Appendix B.

An even more powerful total productivity model aimed at profit-center organizations or whole companies was developed in Houston in the early 1980s by the American Productivity and Quality Center (APQC), which, at that time, was called the American Productivity Center. Building off the concept of relating productivity, profitability, and price recovery, as shown in Table 4.3 on page 54, it provides a vital bridge between the income statement and physical productivity analysis. This model is presented in greater detail in Appendix B.

The APQC model matrix connects change in profitability, productivity, and price recovery with each of the input factors and subfactors. The change is expressed as both an improvement ratio and a dollar effect, which can be interpreted as a *second-order variance*.

FIGURE 5.2. STAIR-STEP USE FUNCTION

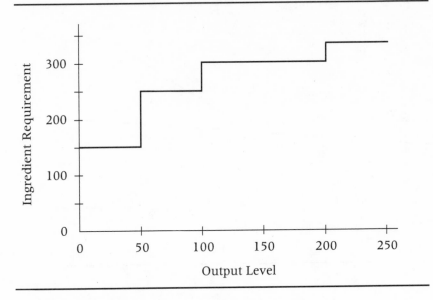

Both factors are necessary because most organizations are interested not only in the factors that show the largest percentage changes but also in the factors that provide the biggest net impact in dollar terms.

Total productivity and total factor productivity data are not for everyone. They tend to go beyond the principle stated earlier that measures should be understandable by the workers who need to act with them. But as part of its strategic planning capability, every major organization should have a model that can provide a big-picture view of the health of the basic business, which can only be expressed through total productivity.

✺ 6 ✺

Productivity and Cost Issues

Until now, we have dealt with well-behaved productivity ratios—physical ratios that routinely produced one kind of output. The real world is full of multiple-output situations, however, with changing production processes, and some of the available data are presented in financial terms. Moreover, the basis of financial accounting is shifting. There is more interest in identifying cost drivers and paying more attention to time—both cycle-time processes and usage time or life cycle of products.

What Is Cost?

As we saw in Chapter 5, productivity can be defined as units of output divided by one or more of the constituent inputs. Product or service cost is all the relevant constituent input costs divided by units of output. Problems with the latter formula arise when organizations have difficulty determining meanings for *relevant* and *unit.*

Relevance depends on one's point of view. A production worker who is familiar with only step 23 of the many steps in the production process directly sees just a few of the costs:

○ The assemblage coming in from step 22,

○ Whatever is added in step 23 in terms of additional materials, machine activity, and the machine's energy and supplies,

○ The people-hours in step 23,

○ Materials handling between step 22 and step 24, and

○ Rework and scrap in step 23 when mistakes are made.

A purely incremental cost, the cost of one additional unit, would include these same costs, but from step 1 to the last step which is usually packaging.

A plant manager would tend to think of incremental as one additional batch or run of perhaps a few hours. He or she would add these additional costs:

○ Plant-fixed costs, such as heating and cooling, security, direct supervision, waste treatment, and utilities, and

○ Order processing, scheduling, storage, packaging, and shipping costs at the plant for a batch.

The business line manager back at headquarters might think of incremental business as being a new customer with special product specifications. Then we are into

○ Customer records and accounting, credit, and salesperson contact,

○ Engineering and product design, and

○ Field service, warranty, and, increasingly, "burial" of fully used products.

Productivity and Cost Issues

As we move higher up in the organization, product costing more and more involves how fixed costs are viewed and allocated. It is argued that no cost is completely fixed. Even the classic fixed cost, the salary of the company president, becomes semifixed as the position expands to become an "office of the president" that includes additional individuals.

Activity-based cost accounting essentially eliminates the concept of overhead.[1] All costs are incurred for a clear reason, and that reason's budget should pay for it. All costs have a driver. Sometimes the driver is additional sales or production volume; then we have traditional variable costs. But often the driver is amount of square footage used or number of product lines, regional offices, suppliers, states operating in, energy use alternatives, new products under investigation, or something else not directly related to volume.

For example, in some businesses, the size of the company's legal department is largely based on the number of state legal jurisdictions in which the company operates, rather than on the volume of legal work done in each state. Thus, when the company expands operations from ten to eleven states, the legal-cost line item for that eleventh state might need to reflect about 9 percent of the total legal department cost, even though sales in the new state are expected to represent only 2 percent of the overall sales volume.

Life-cycle accounting also affects current practice. With this method, the full cost of a product or service, not just the apparent manufacturing cost, is planned to be recovered. Newly considered costs include design customization, field service, and even ultimate disposal, since more and more products are being identified as inappropriate for conventional disposal. For example, ink cartridges from fax and copying machines are now being returned to the manufacturer for disposal, thereby completing their life cycle. Life-cycle costing needs to take such returns into account.

When Henry Ford made only black Model Ts, there wasn't much design cost to allocate on any basis. But with today's mass customization, in some businesses every unit may have its own set of specifications. Though this mass customization is done quite efficiently, often by computer interconnections, each new variation has its own clear and distinct costs.

Though field service contracts are now being sold along with new products, for competitive reasons they don't necessarily cover the full expected service cost. So field-service reserves need to be created out of the product margin. The equivalent of field service can also be found in some service industries. For example, if a guest's hotel stay is marred by a glitch or two, the hotel might offer that guest a free night's stay on the next trip. This type of compensation needs to be accrued.

Weighting of Outputs and Inputs

Let's assume that it matters to you how efficient you are in neighborhood errand running. To gain more insight, you've calculated the duration of your trips to the grocery store by weekday, as shown in Table 6.1. No trips are ever made on Sunday or Wednesday. One tentative conclusion: auto-assemblers syndrome applies to neighborhood errand running; therefore, avoid making Monday trips.

Since a trip to the grocery store actually is a process with multiple outputs, productivity analysis can help decipher the significance of each trip. A trip to the grocery store may just be to the grocery store, but it may also include a trip to the post office and/or a trip to the drug store. In this environment, it is hard to make an accurate

TABLE 6.1. DURATION OF TRIPS TO THE GROCERY STORE

Day of the Week	Duration of Trip
Monday	55 minutes
Tuesday	35 minutes
Thursday	45 minutes
Friday	40 minutes
Saturday	40 minutes

Productivity and Cost Issues

statement about the average duration of trips without some second-order thinking. Let's assume that a month's trip diary revealed the data shown in Table 6.2. Note that something is always needed at the grocery store; there are no trips involving just the drug store or the post office.

TABLE 6.2. ONE MONTH'S TRIP DIARY

Destination	Duration of Trip	Relative Time ("Weights")
Grocery store only	30 min.	1.0
Grocery store and drug store	42 min.	1.4
Grocery store and post office	54 min.	1.8
Grocery store, drug store, and post office	66 min.	2.2

Now we are ready to analyze another month of data (see Table 6.3).

TABLE 6.3. ANOTHER MONTH'S TRIP DIARY

	MONDAYS		ALL OTHER DAYS	
Destination	Number of Trips	Duration in Minutes	Number of Trips	Duration in Minutes
Grocery store only	1	31 min.	10	312 min.
Grocery store and drug store	1	35	15	644
Grocery store and post office	2	114	5	270
Grocery store, drug store, and post office	2	120	1	65
Total	6	300 min.	31	1,291 min.
Average duration of trip		50 min.		42 min.

However, if we track the pattern of the relative time information, setting the historical performance as a standard of sorts, we can weight each destination by giving extra credit for more difficult trips and less credit for easier trips, so that the analysis is much fairer. The standard durations in minutes for the new month are shown in Table 6.4. Thus, Monday's performance of 300 actual minutes' duration is 4 percent better than the standard 312 minutes. And the actual performance for the other days (1,291 minutes) is 2 percent worse than the standard 1,266 minutes. There goes the auto-assemblers' syndrome assumption! When the output mix is taken into account, the data show that performance on Monday is actually a little better than it is during the rest of the week. The new tentative explanation is that Monday's trips include many of the trips to the post office, which is a relatively difficult and therefore time-consuming trip to make.

TABLE 6.4. STANDARD DURATION OF TRIPS FOR NEW MONTH

Destination	Mondays	All Other Days
Grocery store only	30 min.	300 min.
Grocery store and drug store	42	108
Grocery store and post office	108	270
Grocery store, drug store, and post office	132	66
Total	312 min.	1,266 min.

Now let's go on and compare two months' performance using some of the same data and making use of the relative weights calculated above (see Table 6.5). Taking mix into account allows us to make a fair statement about the improvement (3 percent) in errand productivity over the last month.

The failure to recognize hidden mix shift is one of the leading causes of error in productivity analysis. But the type of analysis outlined above can be applied to any multiple-output process in both manufacturing and service industries.

TABLE 6.5. TWO MONTH'S TRIP PERFORMANCE

Destination	FIRST MONTH (Number of trips × weight = weighted trips)	SECOND MONTH Number of trips × weight = weighted trips)
Grocery store	$11 \times 1.0 = 11.0$	$13 \times 1.0 = 13.0$
Grocery store and drug store	$16 \times 1.4 = 22.4$	$15 \times 1.4 = 21.0$
Grocery store and post office	$7 \times 1.8 = 12.6$	$10 \times 1.8 = 18.0$
Grocery store, drug store, and post office	$3 \times 2.2 = \underline{6.6}$	$5 \times 2.2 = \underline{11.0}$
Total	37 52.6	43 63.0
Actual duration of trips	1,591 min.	1,854 min.
Weighted average duration of trips	30.2 min.	29.4 min.

The basis for determining the standards or relative weights can range from a simple historical performance analysis, as above, or an even more informal inspection ("The red ones take about twice as long as the green ones to manufacture"). At the other extreme, a sophisticated weighting system called function points was developed by IBM and some of its key customers in the 1980s to make a generic statement about the relative difficulty of systems programming applications. For each candidate project, prejudgments — simple, average, or complex—were made about five key computer functions—external input, external output, logical internal file, external interface file, and external inquiry. This information was blended with ratings, ranging from 0 to 5, of fourteen other processing-complexity characteristics to come up with an overall complexity weight. With hundreds of observations, multiple regression provided a very good predictor of expected programming hours and a postmeasure of programming productivity, actual versus expected.

So far we've seen how weighting outputs can protect against output mix shift. Although similar techniques can be used to weight inputs, there is usually less need to do so, since inputs can often be adequately protected through price weighting. In labor input, for example, it is true that different types of person-hours may lend themselves more to productive performance than other types. An engineer's hours should be perhaps twice or three times as useful in an engineering project as a secretary's hours. If the engineer is paid about twice or three times as much as the secretary, payroll dollars is, in effect, a self-weighting input. It's in the converse situation, where ability to contribute is grossly unlike pay level, that a supplemental physical weighting system may be needed. If project typing is being done by secretaries and engineers in varying proportions, the secretary hours might be given twice the weight as the engineer's hours to arrive at typing productivity.

Other physical input weighting appears in countless situations, including those involving alternate fuels analysis (as discussed in Chapter 5), alternate vehicles, prime versus less prime warehouse space, different varieties of trees, and different vintages of computer capacity.

Deflation of Cost Elements

When any financial (dollar) costs are compared over time, movement in price or unit cost of the entity represented will hide the underlying physical quantity information. Price effects can be removed using price indices of varying kinds, ranging from homemade approximations to official indices created by trade associations or government agencies. Consider the calculation of materials productivity shown in Table 6.6. Is this decline in materials productivity correct? Consider the additional data provided in Table 6.7.

With this information, it is now possible to calculate Period 2 expenses data in dollars of Year 1. This removes the inflation effect

Productivity and Cost Issues

TABLE 6.6. CALCULATION OF MATERIALS PRODUCTIVITY

	Period 1	Period 2
Weighted units produced	2,340	3,450
Total materials expense	$8,300	$13,800
Units per materials expense	.282	.250
Percent productivity increase or (decrease)	(11.2)%	

TABLE 6.7. ADDITIONAL MATERIALS PRODUCTIVITY DATA

	Period 1	Period 2
Materials expense:		
Steel bar	$6,400	$11,600
Plastics	1,650	1,900
All other materials	250	300
Total Materials Expense	$8,300	$13,800
Steel Producers' Association Price Index	127.9	165.3
Plastic Producers' Association Price Index	176.3	170.0
Producers' price index, all items	109.6	114.3

that's present in Period 2 data. That inflation effect is removed surgically in that each major item, with its own unique price trend, is separately calculated, as shown in Table 6.8.

It would have been possible to bring the Period 1 expenses to Period 2 dollars and make a comparison in Period 2 dollars. In general, the answer would be slightly different but no less "accurate." In fact, the expense data for both periods could be brought to a neutral year or to an arithmetic average of the two sets of index numbers. The use of base-period price weighting, as in the example above, is the normal practice because it allows additional time periods to be added without having to change the indexing mechanism. This moving-forward approach is associated with Laspeyres, a French

TABLE 6.8. PERIOD 2 EXPENSES IN PERIOD 1 DOLLARS

Steel deflation	$11,600 × 127.9/165.3 =	$ 8,975
Plastics deflation	$1,900 × 176.3/170.0 =	$ 1,970
Other items deflation	$300 × 109.6/114.3 =	$ 288
Total deflated expense		$11,233

Recalculated Productivity

	Period 1	Period 2
Weighted units produced	2,340	3,450
Total materials expense (in Period 1 dollars)	$8,300	$11,233
Units per materials expense	.282	.307
Percent productivity increase or (decrease)		8.9%

economist. Current period weighting is more awkward computationally, but working backward from today's actual relative economics is attractive for some purposes. This approach is named after Hermann Paasche, a late nineteenth-century German economist.

The selection of inflation-adjustment indices is somewhat of an art. The basic rule is to get as close as possible to the specific category of product or service without incurring unacceptable cost or complexity. The worst possible deflator is a whole-economy index, such as the Gross National Product deflator or the Consumer (or Producers') Price Index. Of course, if that's all that's available or if an approximation is sufficient, there's a lot to be said for just having to look up the numbers you need on a readily available table.

A good compromise, as used above, is to look for appropriate indices among the regularly published producer price indices of the U.S. Department of Labor and its counterparts in other countries, or similar indices calculated and published by trade associations for their industry. (Producer price indices can be found in *Statistical Abstract of the United States*, published annually by the U.S. Department of Commerce. Monthly updates are found in the *Survey of*

Productivity and Cost Issues

Current Business, also published by the Department of Commerce.) But within any major industry, there can be counter price movements. For example, older products might be stabilizing or even declining in price at the same time that new products are rapidly increasing in price. This can also be true on the input side. Wage rates may be stagnating in low-skill employment at the same time that certain types of technical talent are increasing in wage rate. Forms of energy and types of material may be moving differently. The computer industry, for example, has an unusually wild variation in price direction between different product categories.

The completely controllable solution is to create your own price indices from sales records (for outputs), personnel records (for wage trends), and purchasing records (for other inputs). Although computers allow us to make complex indices that include all inputs or outputs as needed, it is often sufficient to use a sampling basis. For example, a perfectly usable materials price index can be created by tracking the five most often purchased products plus an average of five other randomly chosen products, combined with appropriate weights.

Finally, if general inflation happens to be at a relatively low rate when a measurement system is introduced, don't fail to include the appropriate indexing provisions. Inflation will certainly return.

Contracting In and Contracting Out

With any type of trend analysis, consistency of assumption is absolutely essential for the calculated result to mean anything. Places where consistency is constantly challenged include metal fabrication plants and service industry back rooms. Sometimes an operation is done in-house, and sometimes it's farmed out to a contractor. If the mix of in-house versus farmed-out work stays relatively constant, there's little potential difficulty. But if the mix shifts from period to period, adjustments are required.

Unfortunately, heavy fluctuations are common among organizations that contract out and contract in. Organizations often choose to farm out work because in-house capacity is used up, and this situation tends to arise at odd, somewhat unpredictable intervals rather than regularly. Similarly, extra work is sometimes taken in when another organization unexpectedly can't handle its workload and the organization accepting the work happens to have the appropriate capacity to handle it.

The distortion in analyzing trends in this area comes with the partial productivity ratios, not with the total productivity or total cost. If an organization purchases semifinished components assembled elsewhere, the whole purchase is defined as materials; if assembly is done in-house, the costs affected would be labor, energy, capital, and materials. At the output level, it is indistinguishable which of the upstream production routes was taken, but the labor partial ratio, for example, would automatically show higher labor productivity for the farm-out scenario than for the in-house case.

The same applies to service situations. Let's say the data for a report was self-produced, but in another case, a consulting company was hired to gather it. One cost is called *labor* and the other is called *business services: consultants*. A partial ratio of final reports produced per unit of labor would unfairly favor the consultant route.

Time, the True Bottom Line

For many, the ultimate scarce resource is neither money nor machine capacity nor management talent. It's time. The ancient who said "Time is money" was onto something. As total quality management puts more and more emphasis on the customer, customers have a license to ask for more performance, more customization, lower cost, and shorter order times. Lean/flexible/agile manufacturing starts with the concept that manufacturers must learn how to

Productivity and Cost Issues

supply an often unique product in less time without additional cost—that is, to offer mass customization.

It used to be that on-time delivery was sufficient to ensure customer satisfaction. Elaborate negotiations between the not always completely truthful representatives of supplier and customer set standards and schedules for delivery with elaborate procedures and penalties. But when organizations started budgeting "planned late-delivery payments" and "late-delivery safety stocks," it became clear that there had to be a better way to ensure customer satisfaction.

Shifting to a cycle-time orientation takes away much of the excuse-making capability. As long as everyone in the producing organization could say, "It isn't my fault the product is late; I didn't get all the ingredients until yesterday," lateness would continue to be a problem. But if each person's "clock" doesn't start running until all ingredients are in place, and then great pressure is exerted to provide tools, systems, and training so that the time that each person is the critical factor in the process is reduced, the overall result will be remarkable decreases in overall time from order to delivery.

The literature on quick changeover of manufacturing dies, for example, shows the amazing improvements in cycle time that can occur by planning die changes so that more of the changeover work can be done off-line by regular workers rather than by scarce, expensive, and overloaded specialists. Changeovers that used to take days now take hours, and changeovers that used to take hours now take minutes.[2]

Changeover improvement opportunities can also be found in service industries and support groups. The changing of checkout clerks in a store or the transferring of data from one project group to another follows many of the same issues and principles. Reducing product or service design cycle time also can have a tremendous impact on an organization's competitiveness. Delivering a known competitive product a day earlier than expected may get you a reorder, but offering a new product concept six months before the competition will probably win you a permanent advantage.

From a measurement point of view, it's critical to precisely define the starting and ending points of the cycle and what's included in the product or service deliverables. Some attention should also be given to what sort of "interruptions" or "exceptions" will be adjusted out of trend data and which will be left in. Chaos theory notwithstanding, it's possible to separate includable and excludable traumas.

Measures of Agility

Agility has taken on a meaning of its own in both manufacturing and service industries. The Iacocca Institute of Lehigh University in Bethlehem, Pennsylvania, has led study groups that have gone beyond the lean and flexible concepts of just-in-time production in a high-involvement environment to include such unique features as connectivity and multiventuring.[3]

Connectivity recognizes that the true breakthroughs in cycle-time reduction, considering both the product scheduling and delivery interface as well as the design-manufacturability-customer use interface, come from using interactive computer networking that allows direct adjustment or correction of design online among all relevant parties. Thus, in addition to measuring cycle-time outcomes, there is value in measures of capability to achieve the networking ideal of having all relevant parties up and going on all connectivity vehicles in a user-friendly manner.

Multiventuring (MV) returns us to the basic productivity measures in the sense that the impetus for MV is to avoid the accretion of unnecessary resources in any particular "firm." Each organization that participates in an agile configuration provides *only* what is needed for the project and nothing more. At the end of the project, the configuration dissolves, as do many of the component "virtual" organizations. The directing organization survives to go on to new ventures. Its performance measures will concentrate on measures of leverage; how much end-user value-added is created compared

Productivity and Cost Issues

to the relatively small in-house cost of assembling and managing the project or how many "suppliers" it networks with.

Clearly it's a new world of productivity if there is essentially no labor or capital sitting around waiting for new business. This even raises the possibility of nearly infinite capital productivity organizations and output with no capital required, except a networking computer. Of course, some nonvirtual organizations are stuck with the world's machinery and buildings, but even they will have to start thinking in value-added terms.

SECTION III

The Quality Imperative

An organization's ultimate goal is to satisfy its customers. But doing so requires more than sheer will power and good intentions. In some businesses it's not even easy to identify who the customers are. They come from inside and outside the organization and often make different and even conflicting demands. Therefore, before an organization can attempt to satisfy its customers, it has to make prioritizing its customer-satisfying capabilities a vital part of its planning cycle.

We believe that high levels of customer satisfaction can be reached because excellent organizations periodically tout the stellar results from their customer surveys. But such indicators can be suspect. Heavy response biases can plague even the most carefully conducted surveys. The proliferation of indirect data available to measure customer satisfaction—such as returns, warranty cost, market share, and field performance and maintenance data—must be integrated with survey information to provide a complete picture. But a customer's final word on a product or service is manifested when he or she walks away from your organization and toward another or comes back to you for more.

As they search internally for ways to improve quality, organizations come to realize the importance of identifying and eliminating waste—that is, anything that doesn't add customer value. Some waste, such as excessive materials handling, can't be eliminated without building a completely new plant or system, but other forms of waste, such as changeover time, can typically be greatly improved by the regular workforce without much additional training or investment. As organizations realize the critical role that the workers play in the war on waste, they must look for ways to muster their human resources into work teams and to motivate them to excel. Thus, team effectiveness becomes part of the quality equation and therefore must be measured.

Other measures of quality that enter the picture—innovation, creativity, safety, and behavioral issues—can be analyzed by carefully stating what tangible manifestations are expected when that aspect of quality is present and then "counting" the presence, absence, or even the intensity of that manifestation. That's a tall order to fill, but the quality-driven organization that learns to do so will reap tremendous rewards.

☼ 7 ☼

External Quality: Is the Customer Always Right?

Quality is satisfying the customer. It's as simple—and as difficult—as that.

Productivity zealots would say that customer satisfaction is contained within the idea that outputs are not counted unless they are accepted by the customer. But that's hardly an exciting rallying cry compared to something like, "Quality is the only thing that counts!"

The most common statement used to connect productivity and quality is that productivity is what ultimately makes companies and nations competitive and successful, but that quality is the best way to achieve productivity. This is because quality is better understood and more acceptable to employees, communities, and many other stakeholders than productivity, which has historically been associated with single-minded cost-cutting and efficiency-improvement drives.

Satisfying the customer presents two basic challenges: defining what is meant by *satisfying* and identifying the customer. The first task is easier than the second. In some markets it is still true that "meeting specifications" is satisfying enough to enable an organization to retain its business for the foreseeable future. Or in the monopoly situations that often exist in the public sector and regulated private sector, statutory satisfaction is often viewed as sufficient. But in whim-influenced consumer markets and semicommodity industrial markets, the goal is to "delight" customers, giving them more than they thought was possible. Delighting moves you a step beyond rational analysis and preempts the competition, which is an appropriate concept in any market, as long as it works.

Failed attempts to delight result in unnecessary costs or worse. Intentionally putting 12½ ounces of beer in a 12-ounce beer can may generate enthusiasm among dedicated drinkers if they know about it, but if they don't know about it, the move is tantamount to 4 percent waste. Some people may consider while-you-are-on-hold canned music delightful, but no doubt many others think of it as an unforgivable institutionalization of the hold mode.

Customer Identification

Identifying the customer can be difficult. First, an organization must make the distinction between external customers and internal customers. The main customers of the whole organization and its production processes are external. But the main customers of the production and support sections of an organization are within the organization itself. Since the focus of this chapter is external quality, we will concentrate on external customers.

The first questions to consider in identifying the customer are, "Who does the organization deal with directly? Who uses the organization's products or services? Who is on its mailing list?" A related question might be, "Who pays the bill?" But keep in mind that the bill payer may not be the same person or group as the product or service user. Another useful test is to ask, "Who would be the first to be affected or the first to notice if you stopped doing what you are now doing?"

For manufacturing firms, the ultimate product user is obviously a customer. But there is often also a distributor, wholesaler, or retailer involved upstream from the user. There also may be affected parties downstream from use. In the case of a pollution-control valve used in a manufacturing plant, a valve wholesaler and various plant employees—purchasing agent, engineer, operations manager, and valve installer or maintainer—use the valve. But the plant's neighbors and their enforcement agents also may notice the absence of the valve—perhaps before the plant employees do.

Incidentally, these various customers may not completely agree on what constitutes quality. Everyone wants the valve to work; most everyone wants it to be affordable. The plant people want short order time, ease of installation and maintenance, and long life. The wholesaler wants as much standardization as possible with other similar-use valves and easy storability. The neighbors simply want it to work; to them nothing else matters.

In the public sector, a similar analysis for identifying direct customers applies, but more attention usually is paid to and received from affected parties downstream, both direct enforcers and indirect kibitzers, such as members of Congress and judges.

Since organizations have multiple customers, customer needs must be filtered through a strategic planning process so that management can systematically prioritize its initiatives to satisfy selected customer groups in selected ways.

Direct Measures of Customer Satisfaction

Once customers have been identified, it's possible to get their opinions on both the organization's outputs and its manner of operating. The most common source of direct data is the customer survey, in which customers are asked to rate the organization's products and services in terms of *design* and *delivery*. Assessing both these factors is critical in planning corrective action and employee recognition. An organization cannot redeem a poorly designed product or service simply by having friendly people at the point of failure. Conversely, the benefits that an organization stands to gain from a great product or service design can be lost because of indifferent sales, delivery, or installation.

Whether designed to be answered in writing or over the telephone, the customer survey document must be crafted with great care. Honing in on what the organization needs to know from its customers is not as easy as it sounds. A limited number of seemingly simple questions must yield information on functionality, price, service levels, and even future intentions. Wording must be in the customer's language and yet succeed in separating design issues from delivery issues so the responses will offer the organization real diagnostic value. It is good practice to try out a draft instrument on a group of customers before it is made final to check that it really elicits valuable information.

Frequency is another issue that must be considered when designing customer surveys. Most organizations would like to have customer information frequently—say, monthly. But most individual customers do not want to be bothered answering a survey more than once a year. This is not a problem for mass marketers who have millions of customers to choose from, but organizations with only a few dozen customers may have to settle for surveying one-fourth of their customers each quarter.

Because of systematic bias, surveys shouldn't be the only instrument used to gather customer information. In most survey situations, the displeased are much more likely to respond than the pleased. Although you need to know what the displeased have to say as individuals and correcting problems they report is appropriate, using a biased response as if it were representative of the whole customer population is dangerous. This situation can be avoided by attracting a broader, more representative response base. This can be done by offering customers an incentive to complete the questionnaire or respond to the phone survey, such as a discount on the next purchase or participation in a special lottery for responding customers.

Certifications and awards serve as another direct measure of customer satisfaction. When a supplier moves up a formal step on some customer grid—for example, from submitting a proposal to being shortlisted for a project—that is a reliable indicator of an at least satisfactory relationship. Sometimes such recognition results in the receipt of a greater share of that customer's business. Winning best-supplier awards is also a good sign, but as more and more competitors qualify for those awards, organizations find themselves dealing with the same competition, only at a higher level.

Indirect Measures of Customer Satisfaction

Heading the list of indirect measures is market share. Most organizations, whether manufacturers or service providers, have at least a good idea of their market share in critical products and services and how it is changing. This is not a perfect indicator of satisfaction; customers may be buying now because they see no alternative, but as soon as the competitor's new product is ready or their in-house capability is designed, they may plan to leave you in the lurch. Another problem with market-share data is that it doesn't reflect up-to-the-minute trends. The major market research services often have shorter time lags now than they used to because of bar-coding and EDI capabilities, but in some businesses the lags are still a problem.

For the directorate of any one product line, there is no problem identifying what kind of market-share data is desired. But for a product group or a whole company, indices of market share need to be developed, so simple statements about increase or decrease can be made from complex, multiproduct data. Each product's market share is weighted by relative dollar sales, relative importance at the main production bottleneck, or a subjective "relative importance to our future" concept.

Similar to market share is reorder rate, which is more closely related to how the organization comes out on each purchasing decision, regardless of its size. The reorder rate also may be plagued by a time lag and reflect purchases made for the "wrong" reasons, but when combined with satisfaction survey data, it can provide some solid information. According to some experts, *second-purchase data*, when available, are the best possible data for determining whether an organization is on the right track with a particular product or service.

More indirect but easy to calculate are returns and warranty costs. Not all returns and warranty payments represent true quality failures or customer dissatisfaction. When a retailer finds out that it has overstocked a product, it will use all the leverage it can to return some of the overstock or do some late-night sledgehammer work to generate damaged goods that, in turn, become warranty dollars. Often the supplier's customer representatives know what is happening, and they can check the appropriate box ("overstock" instead of "quality") on their internal control forms. But once a system for analyzing returns has been in place for many years, it can be used to spot new problems before they become pervasive.

In some complex businesses, where customized products or services are the rule, the only really useful customer data come from direct conversation with the customers, either individually or in groups. Focus groups of customers, conducted by outside experts, can be immensely fruitful and unearth the potential for customer dissatisfaction. This sort of information is direct information, but translating it into numbers to use in a measurement system brings it into the indirect category.

Field Performance of Products and Services

In many fields, customer satisfaction is focused on the point of sale, the so-called moment of truth. Certainly with faddish products and most services, that is the appropriate focus. But with durable products, permanent satisfaction of a customer is more appropriately focused on how the product works in the field, how long it lasts, how difficult it is to service, and how much it costs to do so. Some part of warranty cost relates to undoing or revising the point-of-sale action. But another part of warranty cost relates to later field service.

Product-development people often view the "field" as the research laboratory where products are tested and torn down to predict actual performance. This results in quality ratings that are reported to the public in consumer magazines and, in turn, influence buying decisions. Experts differ strongly on the validity and value of such ratings, but regardless of the objective truth about a product, the customer's perception of it is ultimately what counts.

By systematically gathering and analyzing field maintenance records, an organization can come as close to the objective truth about a particular product's performance as possible. However, if such data are gathered only from willing volunteers through, for example, the warranty registration process, the data may be biased. For example, the data might be misleading because the respondents differ from the general populace in the amount of abuse they give the product. Or, more important, the sample can be quite different from the general population in expectations and attitudes. Older Americans expect toasters to last twenty-five years. Younger Americans expect them to last twenty-five months or even less. What is the "true" level of satisfaction here?

Lifetime field performance of a toaster is relatively easy to imagine, including even what "retirement" means for the appliance. But what is the lifetime field performance of an education, a social services intervention, or a preventive health program? When you shift from measuring output to measuring outcome, extra thinking is required.

In education, the output may be a diploma of some sort and the first outcome may be obtaining a job. But as time passes, other outcomes come into play. Can the diplomate make the transition from first job to second job, whether in the same organization or not? Is the diplomate an effective member of the community? In other words, can that person apply the education received beyond his or her work specialty? This is one reason that communities offer continuing education programs, even though they never refer to them as field maintenance.

The Ultimate External Customer

An organization's ultimate external customer is the community in which it operates or exerts influence. Although the quality of the organization's relations with the community may not be considered one of its key processes, those relations will need to be measured by public relations executives and staff.

The family-of-measures concept fits well within the community context. Political balance is what holds a community together; different interests form temporary coalitions to get things done. A balance is struck between different "good things" so everyone is partly pleased. Progress consists of balanced progress toward an array of goals. Community quality statements are usually followed by lists of examples of progress on many fronts. The occasional community ratings are usually an index of fifteen to twenty desirables, and the winner is usually the one that finishes in the top quarter on nearly everything rather than the one that finishes first on only one thing.

An important bridge to the community, for good or ill, is the environmental effects of the organization on the community. When assessing environmental quality, once again, a family-of-measures approach works well.[1] Although legislation may be drafted to protect the environment by allowing only a specific percentage of a particular chemical in the air, community members realize that environmental quality is a combination of many kinds of annoyances being present or absent. We talk of the balance of nature as automatically directing long-term biological change. That balancing act must be maintained as human beings—individually or in groups—exert their influence. Their effects on the community and its environment should be measured as a quality index, reflecting the varying annoyances properly weighted by the affected parties.

❖ 8 ❖

Internal Quality: The Search for Waste

Although the place most people start looking for quality of product or service is at the moment of truth and beyond (field maintenance), the reason quality exists is that appropriate things were done earlier in the design and production of the product or service. A smiling bank teller doesn't offset the fact that the teller's screen is blank because of an upstream failure. An athlete's performance on the field is partly determined by what was learned and practiced in training camp.

The facts represented by customer satisfaction or dissatisfaction are important to register, understand, and monitor, but the diagnostic value of those facts is what's really important. What has the organization learned that will enable it to prevent the deviation from intended practice from happening again? In many cases, deviation occurs upstream in the production process. One of the major quality analysis techniques, quality function deployment, is based on the idea of reasoning backward from the customer, back upstream, to connect customer needs to internal practice insufficiencies.

The Organizational War on Waste

"All materials handling is waste!"

This isn't a comforting message for a diligent materials-handling manager to hear. He or she works hard to see that each part of the production process has what it needs when it needs it. Much time is spent debating the best kinds of conveyors and lift trucks, not to mention warehouse carousels and automatic guided vehicles. How can all that be wasteful?

Of course, it all depends on your point of view. What Shigeo Shingo, the late Japanese coinventor of the Toyota production process, meant by the quote above is that if an organization is able to start over and create a new production process, it should be a just-in-time process where material enters production only when it's needed. It should flow unimpeded directly through each succeeding process step until the product is ready to be shipped. Each process step should be located next to the preceding one and dedicated only to that particular process. That would eliminate most of the modern organization's materials-handling problems.

But most organizations don't have the luxury of starting over, so they do the best they can with the layout and general workflow that they inherit. In this case, it's possible to talk about the "best" way to handle materials, move them more quickly, to have them more clearly marked, and to discourage interruption and hesitation in routing. Nevertheless, everyone should stay alert to the possibility of rethinking methods and challenging basic assumptions about any so-called normal or usual materials-handling processes.

Shingo's Seven Wastes

Shingo identified seven overlapping types of waste in a production environment.[1] Many of these also apply to service industries and support processes within any industry that take a broad view of "production." Shingo's seven wastes are as follows:

1. Defects

It is clearly wasteful to make a product or provide a service that doesn't meet specifications. A defective part must be thrown away or reworked, both of which cost the organization extra money. A service call that doesn't take care of a particular problem must be repeated.

2. Overproduction

In the days when economies of scale was the dominant manufacturing model, expensive and scarce machines were kept running longer than necessary to produce enough products to meet current customer demand so that machine hours would not be wasted. The extra parts or products that resulted were viewed benignly because it was thought that someday there might be a surge in demand and the extra parts or products would be there, ready to go. Any extra costs incurred under this system—such as interest, storage space, obsolescence, and the like—could be covered by raising the price a few cents. But in today's organization, "someday" never comes. Production schedules exactly meet demand; they produce neither more nor fewer products than needed.

Overproduction isn't unique to the factory setting. Let's say an office needs about 100 copies of a new report. But the second hundred costs only 60 percent of the cost of the first hundred. This is a bargain the organization can't miss, reasons the office manager, since it lowers the apparent unit cost by 20 percent. Unfortunately, the extra copies will probably be floating around that office long after most of the employees have gone on to greener pastures.

3. Waiting Time

There are still plants in which 90 percent or more of the elapsed time from receipt of order to shipping is spent with the budding product or service order waiting for the next processing step. There is such a thing as *curing time* for some products or *verification time*, but in most cases the waiting time is not a process specification but, rather, a process accident. The main culprit is mandatory large batches on critical machines (to avoid changeover costs from product to product) that cause all the other components to wait so they can all flow downstream together.

4. Transport Time

Everything else being equal, it's obviously better to transport intermediate goods less often rather than more often. For large or odd-shaped things, transport requires expensive vehicles and resting or storage space. For smaller things or liquids, the main direct cost is a conduit, such as a pipe, or conveyor belts. For very small components, the need to transport them hundreds of feet instead of a few inches because of an inefficient layout may force batch treatment and eliminate the possibility of continuous flow. Every additional unit of time required because of transport increases the amount of work-in-process inventory in the system. Transport time is a significant factor in many service and support applications where paper is physically moved. But in other service applications, transport time is reduced to zero by the use of electronic networks or to nearly zero by the fax machine.

5. Processing

Processing waste often comes in the form of materials scrap. Unplanned scrap is considered a defect, but planned scrap may also be unnecessary. If the raw material comes only in certain sizes and shapes, a cutting plan is established to minimize waste, but it may have been possible to choose an even less wasteful pattern or work with the supplier to come up with a less wasteful size. The speed of the machine may also lead to waste. If it is set too slow, the machine may become a bottleneck. It can also be wasteful if the machine is set too fast in a situation where the operator would be able to handle two slower-moving machines as easily as one fast-moving machine.

6. Excess Inventory

Most of the other forms of waste generate unnecessary inventory, whether stocks of defects awaiting rework, overproduction waiting to fit in a schedule, or full conveyor belts or surge tanks. Some excess inventory, especially as raw material or finished goods, may be present for marketing reasons. Perhaps the purchasing department made an unusually good deal on a raw material, so it was bought or delivered before the time of need. Or perhaps a customer will accept only a certain minimum-quantity delivery, which requires the organization to accumulate the product. But there is rarely justification for work-in-process inventory cluttering the plant once a fully integrated, flexible manufacturing system has been established.

Of course, support areas are notorious for high work-in-process inventories, too, although this waste never enters the accounting system. As downsizing occurs in support areas, more and more projects sit on people's desks in various stages of partial completion, waiting for them to find the time to finish them. As with direct production, it might have been better never to have accepted the order if the capacity wasn't available to be able to schedule the work to meet the deadline. The problem is that "capacity" isn't as clearly defined in support areas as it is on the factory floor.

7. Excess Motion

This factor was probably overanalyzed in the past but may be underanalyzed now. The famous engineer's stopwatch has been banished from most companies, but many workers—whether they operate a large machine or simply a phone and computer—waste much time in their routine operations. Simple devices—such as color-coding or marking in tape the "official" resting place of a stapler or calculator—can save tiny amounts of time but saved over and over and over again lead to significant time savings in the long run. Organizing the files better, whether electronic or paper, can save time and avoid great disruption and frustration. Even making breaks more efficient isn't as bad as it sounds. For example, the seemingly simple coffee-making process is a major stumbling block in many offices, with disputes arising from such concerns as where the coffee is made and by whom and in what kind of containers it's consumed. Likewise, well-intentioned recycling efforts have become major generators of excess motion among both high-priced staff and the night crew.

The Key Measure of Internal Quality

Shingo's goal was to turn all other kinds of waste into waiting time because waiting time is the most visible waste. Idle machines, boxes of inventory, and idle people would, no doubt, attract the attention of management and workers alike, allowing prolem-solving teams to get off to a clearer start. The system is challenged each time an improvement is made in eliminating any of the wastes, and new bottlenecks are found that, in turn, need to be worked on.

This is why process cycle time is the key measure of internal quality. Nothing else that can be measured has the comprehensive power to reflect all the forms of waste in the organization. Reducing process cycle time normally also reduces costs, since it eliminates non-value-added activity of all sorts. Certain aspects of quality are also improved as cycle time is reduced. The obsolescence risk is essentially eliminated because nothing stays around long enough to become outdated. Many "wrong part" errors can be eliminated when the part flows in just-in-time for immediate use rather than being pulled from one of a number of similar-looking bins.

The aspect of quality that needs the most attention while efforts are being made to reduce cycle time is retention of the integrity of the individual workers' tasks. Just-in-time systems may seem to generate immense pressure on line workers to *not* be the one to hold up everyone else, but, in fact, those systems authorize every worker to stop the whole line rather than pass on a bad unit. As noted in the discussion of waste factor 3 above, some 90 percent of work is non-value-added waiting time, which can largely be eliminated. Therefore, there is little need to try to reduce the remaining 10 percent that is actual process time. Overall cycle-time-reduction projects sometimes result in an increase in hands-on time and a consequent improvement in the physical quality of the product.

Measuring Cycle Time

Computers have made cycle-time measurement a lot easier than it used to be. Although the external customer might have been given an estimate of normal cycle time, the only way actual data were obtained was by physically tracking units through the plant as they were being assembled. For example, a large casting informally tagged with a green chalk mark entered the production process by itself and ended up as part of an engine twenty-seven days later. All that was necessary to determine cycle time was to define the starting point—when the casting entered production—and the end point—when shipping documents were taped to the engine.

Today, a couple of swipes of a bar-code wand do the same job. Organizations are no longer dependent on occasional cycle-time samples but can count their entire production and apply statistical process control techniques to determine the cycle-time variation. Unusual cycle times can be studied for special causes versus normal variation, and the effects from special causes can be eliminated. Normal variation can also be reduced once it's understood.

In more complex processes, the starting point may vary, depending on the situation. Sometimes the identifying tag needs to be put on a connecting rod, a can of paint, or even the final packing material because that is where the current delivery problems or machining problems are found.

In service industries and support groups, where to put the "green chalk mark" is clear: there's a formal request or order, or someone comes through the door. The problem here lies in sufficiently generalizing the definition of the process. Among social workers, each case is different. The only common processes may appear to be very small parts of the overall effort, such as filling out certain forms or delivering a bag of groceries. Even the end point may not be clear. When can the social worker declare the case to be finished, solved, or cured? Usually only the workers themselves can come up with the required generalizations; only they truly understand all that is happening. The "treatment," however, may be defined—for example, as the time from the moment the case subject agreed to be helped through the time when the subject showed progress in taking a self-help initiative.

Internal Customer Satisfaction

Reducing overall cycle time helps satisfy the external customer and brings with it cost savings and tangible product quality improvements. But there is also a group of internal customers who are looking for satisfaction. This group is made up of all employees of the organization. Everyone is the customer of at least a few other employees of the organization, just as nearly everyone is a supplier to others within the organization. Even salespeople, who may seem to be supplying outsiders only, supply secondary products—sales data, sales promotion advice, competitor intelligence—to insiders. The purchasing specialists, who may be thought to have only external suppliers, are, in fact, supplied with a great deal of data on desired specifications, other new suppliers, and schedule alternatives by other insiders.

Each individual at each step of the internal process flow is interested in receiving materials or ideas from his or her internal suppliers on time, with all functions intact, and proper documentation, all in the proper quantity. So families of measures that deal with the different aspects of internal quality and provide information to help the downstream people manage their part of the business can be created along each identified key process. This information can be communicated on bulletin boards, through regular meetings, electronically, or even within the physical bundles of documentation that accompany the flow of the product or service.

Clearly the development of these process-oriented families of measures requires maximum participation from upstream workers, downstream workers, and the various monitors that may be established in addition to functional specialists, such as accountants and human resources specialists.

Measures of Team Effectiveness

Organizations that aim to please their internal customers usually develop natural work teams to routinely manage their part of a horizontal process. Thus, measures of internal customer satisfaction are important to measures of team effectiveness. In general terms, a team is effective if it scores highly in three areas:[2]

1. Satisfying its customers (as perceived by those customers),

2. Efficiently accomplishing what it's assigned to do, and

3. Functioning well as a team (as determined by the team).

In an integrated and well-coordinated organization, the goals of the first two areas should be very much alike, but they won't necessarily be identical. The most common divergence stems from cost constraints in the assignment that are not known to the downstream customers. For example, let's say a marketing team is asked to create a dynamic brochure for the salesforce to use in promoting a new product. If there were an unlimited budget, that assignment wouldn't be difficult. But if the assignment includes a cost constraint, the team has a much tougher job to do.

Or consider an unimaginative senior manager who assigns a training development team to create a traditional classroom training program to teach maintenance parameters on a new machine. The team creates exactly what was asked for, but the maintenance people have heard of video-based job-site programs for the new machine and wonder why their training doesn't take this better approach. As these examples show, completing a team assignment is not necessarily synonymous with satisfying the team's customers.

As teams mature, team-like functioning, satisfaction, and accomplishment are more likely to go together, but in the early teamwork days they are sometimes quite different. For example, it could be that as long as a team's resident software expert handled a particular aspect of a computer application program, it was done well, but when the team members started alternating duties, it sometimes got messed up. Or when the team was heavily coached on work sequences, it remained efficient, but whenever it set up its own sequences, they bombed with customers.

When it comes to assessing a team's performance, organizations are tempted to waffle on the criteria for top-flight functioning. "I'll know good teamwork when I see it," goes the reasoning. But it is possible to be quite specific regarding proper team functioning. Some measures of a team's performance include

- Multijob capability and certification,

- Level at which certain decisions are made,

- Attendance, absenteeism, and turnover,

- Suggestions and modifications in process,

- Training intensity and skill retention,

- Utilization of assigned tools,

- Housekeeping and documentation discipline, and

- Legitimate external boasting about accomplishments.

The Cost of Poor Quality

So far, all the quality data discussed, both internal and external, have been physical data that can be expressed in rates, percents, or units of time or with a yes or no response. Underlying all this is the ability to translate everything to financial terms and arrive at the cost of doing things wrong. Armand V. Feigenbaum, Philip Crosby, and other quality experts have developed a method for bringing together all the types of failures and inadequacies of an organization using the common denominator of unnecessary cost dollars incurred.[3] Starting from a baseline of a hypothetically perfect organization that does the right things right the first time, the actual gap between this baseline and current performance is calculated and valued in dollars. The categories of failures are expressed in different terms by different authors, but they include those shown in Table 8.1.

TABLE 8.1. CATEGORIES OF POOR QUALITY

ternal Nonconformance	External Nonconformance	Costs of Conformance
:rap	Warranty costs	Quality training
ework, repair, and retest	Quality complaint handling	Vendor certification
uality-caused downtime	Returns and recalls	Quality teams administration
nplanned maintenance downtime	Return freight	Preventive maintenance
ngineering errors	Sales errors	Design reviews
xcess inventory	Unplanned discounts and concessions	Inspection costs
ut-of-spec purchased materials	Quality-related overdue receivables	Market surveys
	Sales lost due to poor quality performance or reputation	Standards development

At first glance, the last category—cost of conformance—might seem out of place because it's composed of "good things" for an organization to do. But a perfect organization would have already done these things, rendering most of them no longer needed. Even a perfect organization (if there could ever be such a thing) would have to incur some training, maintenance, review, and survey costs, but not very much.

When all the cost of performance gaps are added, the result is dollar-departure-from-quality numbers that can be directly ratioed to dollars of total cost or dollars of sales. The resulting percent is nearly always larger than expected and can serve as a powerful wake-up call to senior managers who previously were not believers in the importance of quality. When the cost of quality is represented as being less than 10 percent of sales, it's usually found that an insufficiently broad definition of inadequacy was used. Even so-called world-class organizations are not that good—yet! If a serious job is done of quantifying the value of customers lost because of quality failures, it's easy to get over 30 percent of sales in both manufacturing and service companies. Companies with very high reputations can be found in the 15 to 25 percent range, but wide variations are possible from industry to industry.

Once cost-of-quality data have served their purpose to heighten quality awareness, they can be broken down and used for diagnosis and prevention initiatives. If the senior executives are already believers, the dollarization and aggregation aren't necessary. There's plenty of diagnostic power residing directly in the underlying physical data. But you never know where a nonbeliever might be lurking!

The Seven Problem-Solving Tools

The emphasis so far has been on relatively big pictures—the whole organization, the department, key processes, and teams. But much of the history of quality measurement has been at a still more micro level—the individual work station or machine. Here measurement is easy to understand, certainly challenging to interpret properly, but not necessarily easy to do. Modern quality advocates have found great success in organizing and presenting data in special ways to improve the ability to analyze that data clearly. Each merits some discussion.

Checksheet

The *checksheet* is a running log that sorts occurrences by a simple characteristic or two. This is the basis of all micro quality measurement; it answers the question, "What's happening?" Very often this sort of data generates an immediate solution without further analysis. All it takes is a little systematic data to isolate an unusual effect, as in Table 8.2's source of high food inventory. Of course, honest reporting is assumed.

TABLE 8.2. CHECKSHEET: SOURCE OF HIGH FOOD INVENTORY

	PURCHASES BY SHOPPER (JUNE AND JULY)					
Items in Surplus	*Dad*	*Mom*	*Grandpa*	*Son*	*Daughter*	*Total*
Ice Cream	I	II	II	卌		10
Lettuce	I	III			IIII	8
Potato chips	II	III		III	IIII	12
Kiwi fruit		卌				5
Cat food	I	I			卌	7
Pickled herring		I	III			4

Line Graph

A *line graph* usually is used to identify time trends and show component data together with aggregated data. In Figure 8.1 on page 115, the two components tell a much more interesting story about the number of employees at Acme than the aggregated trend.

FIGURE 8.1. LINE GRAPH: NUMBER OF EMPLOYEES AT ACME

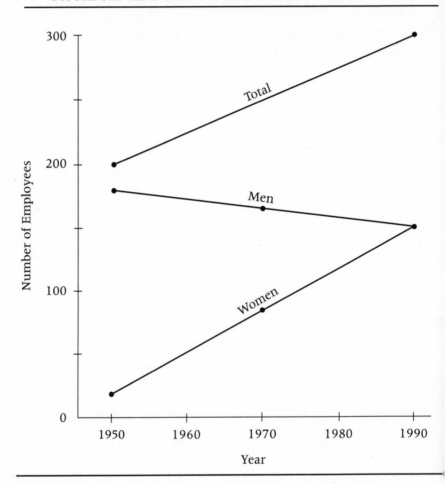

Histogram

A *histogram* is a set of vertical bar graphs that demonstrates the distribution of a variable in a population. Whether it is "normal" or skewed in some direction, the general distribution of the population is quickly apparent in a histogram. In Figure 8.2A, the guests at a children's basketball camp appear to be a normal group of adults, whereas Figure 8.2B shows the coaches and players, quite a different group.

FIGURE 8.2. HISTOGRAMS: PEOPLE AT BASKETBALL CAMP

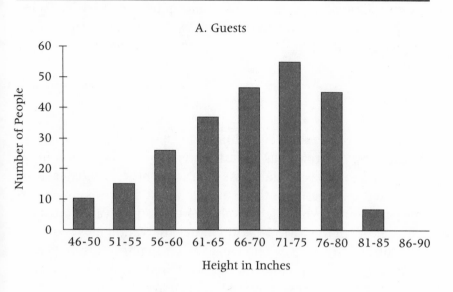

A. Guests

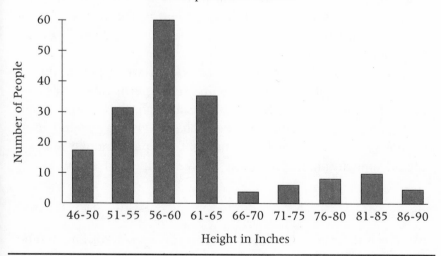

B. Participants and Coaches

Scatter Diagram

A *scatter diagram* analyzes the relationship between two variables. The profit versus productivity diagrams in Chapter 4 showed no apparent relationship. Figure 8.3 in constrast, depicts quite a solid relationship.

Control Chart

The *control chart* is the key technique in statistical process control (SPC). Here, control limits are calculated based on variation information from the basic data set. As long as the process variable being monitored stays between the control limits, it can be assumed that any variation can be safely explained as normal variation that's consistent with the basic data. But if the observation moves outside the control limits, you can no longer assert that the current performance is normal; something has changed in the process, making it, in effect, a new process. Control has been lost. The measured variable can be a physical dimension, with control limits set at, say, a diameter of 2.04 to 2.10 inches, as shown in Figure 8.4. But the measured variable can also be a binary function, such as "it works" or "it doesn't work."

According to a school of thought associated with Japanese quality expert Kaoru Ishikawa, control limits are too permissive. The better discipline, he contends, is to focus on a single-point target value, with any variation from that being bad. This may sound more expensive to achieve, but with the right equipment and training, it can become automatic and bring a huge competitive advantage.

Pareto Chart

In a *Pareto chart*, a collection of errors is classified according to type. Vilfredo Pareto, a late nineteenth-century Italian economist, observed that in many cases, a great amount (up to 80 percent) of the difficulty with a process was caused by a relatively small number (say 20 percent) of potential causes. For example, 80 percent of

FIGURE 8.3. SCATTER DIAGRAM: DOGS AND THEIR OWNERS
AT STYLE KENNELS

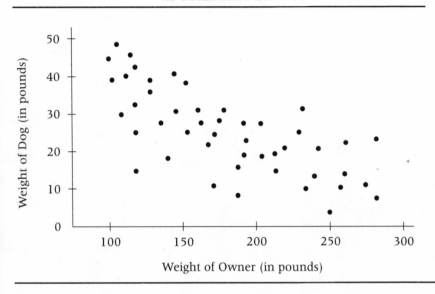

FIGURE 8.4. CONTROL CHART: ZOG DIAMETER VARIATION

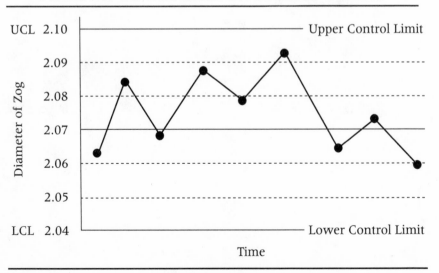

classroom disruptions are caused by 20 percent of the pupils, 80 percent of typing errors involve 20 percent of the keys, and so on. Figure 8.5 makes it quite clear where the Cubs should concentrate their improvement efforts.

FIGURE 8.5. PARETO CHART: WHY THE CUBS FAILED

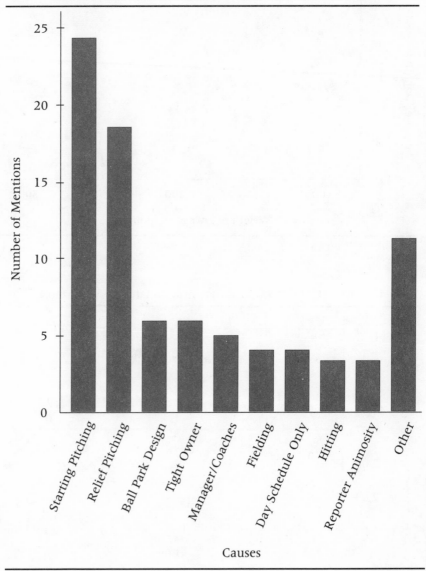

Internal Quality: The Search for Waste

Cause-and-Effect Diagram

In a *cause-and-effect diagram*, also known as a *fishbone chart*, an identified problem is driven "backward" as to potential causes based on the experience of a group of people familiar with the problem. In Figure 8.6, the categories of potential causes at the Paradise Restaurant are people, materials, and equipment. In other applications, the causes may be more fundamental—problems with the process design or even with the product or service concept itself.

☼

Although they aren't exactly measurement tools, these seven tools help the user determine precisely what needs to be measured to prove or disprove a hypothetical problem solution. Measurement is useless if it doesn't provide focus toward improvement. That is what these quality tools do.

When the ancient Greek philosopher Democritus said, "I would rather discover one cause than gain the kingdom of Persia," he was staking out a position as an early quality measurer that we can still identify with today. Just as the historical core of productivity analysis is to streamline production processes by identifying steps and tasks and reducing their complexity, so the historical core of quality analysis is to reduce variation and consequent waste in the elemental parts of the production process. Clearly both are needed. There's no point in reducing variation within a step that's unnecessary in terms of adding value for the customer. It's insufficient to streamline a process at the "steps" level and not apply the same degree of attention to the waste within each step. And the key to ensuring both productivity and quality is capturing the attention and loyalty of the people throughout the organization, so that they can take the lead in streamlining the organization's processes and reducing variation and waste.

Figure 8.6. Cause-and-Effect Diagram: Paradise Restaurant

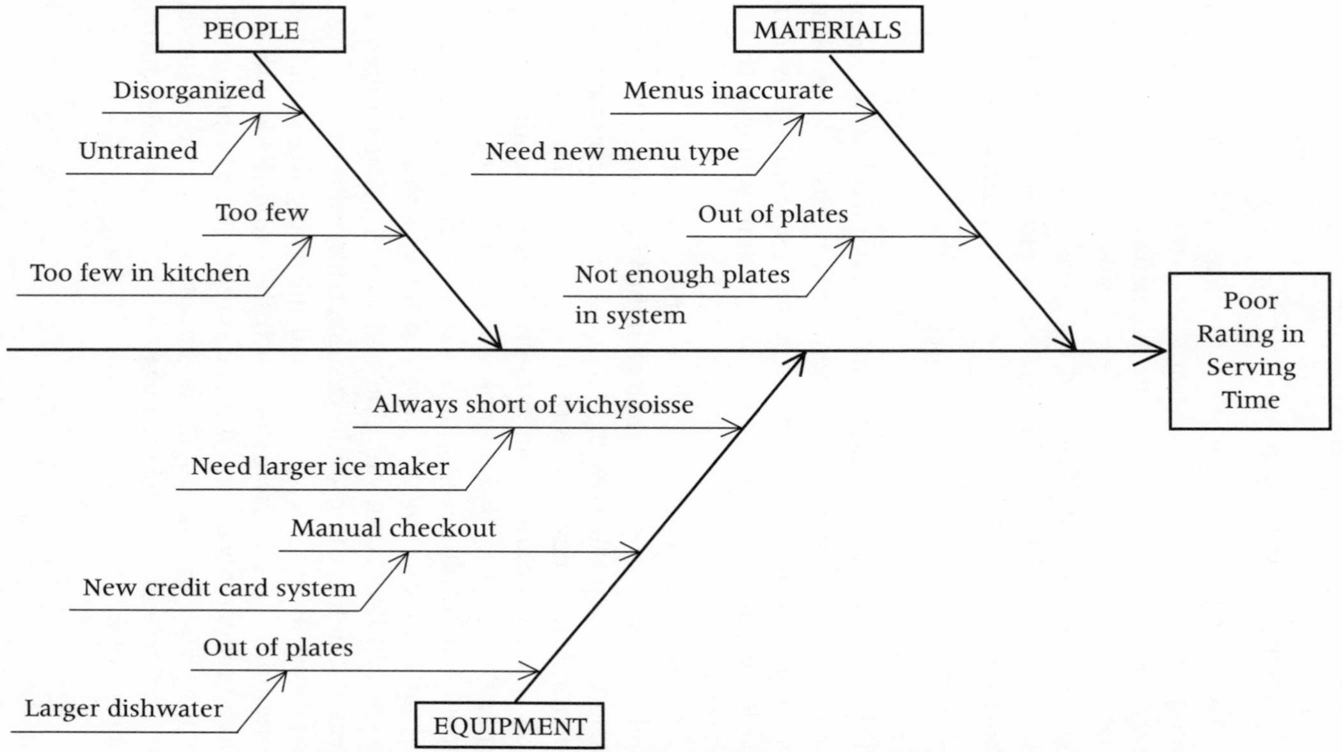

☼ 9 ☼

More Quality Measures: "I'll Know It When I See It!"

An advertising agency or research laboratory must be concerned with creativity. Auditors and bank tellers are preoccupied with documentation. Explosives manufacturers had better pay great attention to safety. Although productivity, quality, and customer satisfaction are the predominant performance measurement categories in most organizations, they are far from the only important measures. Even if the big three dominate at the top of an organization, somewhere lower in the organization are groups and processes where other variables are of equal importance and have major potential for improvement.

Innovation and Creativity

Although every organization professes to encourage innovation and creativity, the terms are used so broadly that they are useless when referring to day-to-day management issues. The word *innova-*

tion contains the Latin root word for *new—novus—*implying a new way of doing things. An innovation in one organization might be a simple change that others elsewhere have been doing for a long time. Thus, measuring innovation is measuring the degree of change, an important but relatively simple concept. For example, if an organization that historically tended to develop and promote its people within the same division—or *silo* on the organizational chart—suddenly starts encouraging cross-silo transfers, it is making an innovative move. Cross-silo transfers divided by all transfers would be a measure of that organization's innovation.

Creativity, on the other hand, is defined in terms of imagination and inventiveness. A creative solution may never have been seen before. Its elements may be simple, but simple things juxtaposed strangely or presented in a different style or order are creative. For example, the development of therapeutically useful combinations of simple chemicals could be part of a creativity measure.

Most *poke-yoke* (mistake-proofing) devices developed by the workforce in a factory represent both innovation and creativity.[1] Take a situation where workers have to reach into an array of twenty-four pigeon holes containing nuts and bolts to get the right hardware for a constantly changing set of products rolling by. The standard practice in this facility would be for workers to read the product number, find the matching pigeon hole by number, pick out the correct nut and bolt, and insert them into the product, with an elapsed time of about twenty to twenty-five seconds per unit and a 5 to 10 percent error rate. To improve the process, the work team could design a color-coded template for the array of pigeon holes, so all the workers would have to do to make sure they got the right hardware was to glance at the color code of the product and apply a template of the same color that would mask all but the right pigeon hole. The insertion operation now might take only ten seconds and be foolproof! To say this improvement merely represents an innova-tion or change is to understate its character; it is also a highly creative application.

Formal measurement of innovation and creativity aims at intentional or planned change and problem solving. Some creativity or, more properly, invention occurs by accident. It's the unusual organization that can successfully plan its accidents, but occasionally research organizations will purposely put together wildly differing types of people and charge the group with a challenging problem. A university or a research hospital could measure the percentage of its projects that were cross-disciplinary in the sense that members of more than one department or section participated.

In the more obscure areas of mental activity, it almost takes a creative person to know one. In other words, only a brain surgeon can understand and, thus, measure the creativity of another brain surgeon. Only a poet can measure the creativity of a poet. The only way someone who's not a brain surgeon or a poet can enter those realms is to carefully gather information or opinions on the tangible manifestation of creativity in that field. A creativity analyst has to ask experts what makes practitioner A more creative than practitioner B. Can differences be noted in the outcome of their work? In their manner of working? In their manner of preparation?

This question-asking approach leads to the identification of "surrogate" measures of creativity. For example, universities measure the creativity of a professor by his or her number (or even pages) of refereed journal output. Ad agencies measure their creativity by their work's appearance on the most remembered ads list and by market-share increase for the advertised product or service. Pharmaceutical laboratories calculate the percentage of the sales of current products developed in their own laboratories (as opposed to licensed or stolen). They also calculate the percentage of sales of self-developed products in the last five years. Symphony orchestras calculate the percentage of played debut pieces and works from a certain period and from a certain part of the world.

Creativity measurement is basically an attempt to be more specific than "I'll know it when I see it" when analyzing intangibles. If the tangible manifestation of creativity in a given situation can be identified, then creativity can be indirectly measured.[2]

Documentation

Documentation is often viewed as a nuisance, but sometimes there's good reason for the existence of the documentation other than to affix blame if something goes wrong. The whole product warranty system, for example, depends on a paper track or an electronic equivalent to establish purchase date and agreed-upon terms, the procedures for subsequent repairs and complaints, and the reason for the current complaint. Most medical research and some medical treatment depend heavily on the accuracy and promptness of both historical and current information.

Both accuracy and timeliness of documentation need to be measured because there's somewhat of a tradeoff between the two. When response must be quick, there's a risk of inaccuracy. A requirement for precise quality may introduce delay into the system. A pathology lab will do a better job of judging the malignancy of a tumor if it can apply several tests taking hours or even days to complete than if the results are needed immediately because the patient is already being operated on. But in the latter case, a quick decision is required, even if it's based on an educated guess.[3]

In some cases, an organization is doing its job regarding documentation if it simply provides access. The old concept of "need to know," which kept most information (whether important or not) in relatively few hands, meant those entrusted with the information had responsibility and power. Documentation that's both timely and accurate is useless if the person who can act upon it doesn't know where it's kept or is bureaucratically prohibited direct access. The other side of the coin is that if no one in particular is responsible for maintaining a certain data base or set of files, it will gradually become inaccurate and out of date.

How does an organization measure its documentation efforts? It's not difficult to measure errors per document, late filings against total filings, or number of files "completed." But these measures should be featured in a family of measures only if they are of real importance. There's sometimes a strong temptation for an organization's managers to choose easy measures over important ones.

Safety and Housekeeping

It's almost impossible for an organization, especially a manufacturer, to keep safety off its list of five or six key performance indicators. In organizations with good safety records where the measurement philosophy is to highlight the measure they most want to improve, safety will simply need to be maintained. Some safety-critical parts of a plant may choose safety as one of their primary measures, but further safety improvement may not be considered vital to the plant as a whole.

One reason safety is sometimes left off the list of principal indicators is that it's not easy to measure. The key word for ensuring safety (as it is for ensuring quality) is *prevention*. An organization would like to measure *units of prevention*, but that's almost as difficult to measure as units of readiness in the air force. Thus, you measure outcomes, either injuries or reportable incidents, per employee or time period. Precision also requires a weighting system that takes seriousness of incident or injury into consideration. But such a system may lead to a meaningless evaluation, since every unsafe practice is potentially serious, even if the reported outcome this time was minor.

Housekeeping is much like safety; it's mainly noticed after a problem has occurred. In a controlled laboratory setting, for example, it goes unnoticed until some product has to be destroyed because of contamination. To try to get ahead of the situation, some organizations slap workers with demerits for very minor violations of strict procedures to "teach them a lesson." But as with fire drills, the motivation that this tactic engenders tends to wear off after several false alarms.

Behavioral Variables

An organization will sometimes try to measure certain aspects of its culture, not usually as a routine performance measure but for a special project to determine whether some cultural innovation is "taking hold." The most commonly surveyed behavioral variable is employee attitude. Usually, employees are asked to fill out surveys on how they view their workplace, the organization, its management style, and their prospects for the future. Clearly, this can't be done routinely or the respondents will get into a self-fulfilling loop. Believing their duty to be to demonstrate "improved" attitudes, they'll fill out followup surveys accordingly.

Certain parts of the organization have a legitimate need to measure behavioral variables. Anything that can be learned about external customers' perception of degree of trust and integrity in the supplier-customer relationship is important to know. The functioning of internal teams depends heavily on the feeling that they're being trusted and empowered by management to deliver the right result, and they want to be valued for their ability to work well as a team. The public relations staff will occasionally need to know how the organization is perceived in the community, especially if the organization has, for better or for worse, been the subject of newspaper or television news reports.

Most good measurement of intangibles, such as behavioral variables, has to concentrate on the carefully considered tangible manifestations of the target behavior rather than on the behavior itself. For example, since some people say that they choose their hair stylist based on that person's "empathy" rather than either measured skill or availability, the thickness of a particular stylist's appointment book could be a tangible manifestation of that stylist's empathy. Some tangible manifestations of behavioral variables in an organization are shown in Table 9.1.

TABLE 9.1. MANIFESTATIONS OF BEHAVIORAL VARIABLES

Behavioral Variable	Tangible Manifestation
Organizational flexibility	Thickness of procedure or personnel manual
Trust	Median distance from the boss's office to subordinates' offices
Organizational openness	Percentage of wall-less offices
Responsibility	Percentage of salaried workers leaving more than one hour after closing
Thriftiness	Percentage of computer terminals routinely used by more than one person

The Marketplace

Another bottom-line consideration besides profit is market acceptance. In some industries, a public testing, reviewing, or survey organization rates different products or services. To have the "best" product from a testing organization is very good. To have the "best" product as seen by the buyers of your product is bliss! Such a result doesn't necessarily spell complete success, however. Complacency must be avoided, and workers and managers alike must realize that today's hero product or service sets high expectations that can quickly be brought down by only one highly publicized crash. There's also danger in assuming that success in one market—whether geographic, demographic, or ethnic—will guarantee success in another.

Most organizations measure market share of their major products and services. As emphasized in Chapter 7, market-share data have the most diagnostic value when they're used as a measure for the marketing and product management groups in the middle of the organization, where they can be assessed in terms of individual products and markets rather than as an overall indicator. Nonetheless, the organization's top management will often want some type of overall index that gives "average market share" of a number of their products or services.

Special Profiles

The essence of good management is to keep a large number of variables in balance. That, too, is the philosophy behind the family of measures concept. The variables discussed in previous chapters—productivity, quality, customer satisfaction—are the obvious variables to consider. But each manager has his or her own additional pulse points to monitor. Many of these points represent a particular mix to keep in balance.

Product Mix

Is there a good balance between low- and high-priced versions, older and newer versions, summer and winter versions, and so on?

Work Mix

When the balanced product requirements are translated back to factory or service-center capacities and capabilities, is the organization playing to its upstream strengths? A company whose strength is management of automation shouldn't be soliciting business that requires much handwork elaboration.

Customer Mix

Even with the right product mix, the organization could have the wrong customer mix. Selling upscale products in low-scale stores isn't a viable long-term strategy. If, for example, an onion rings purveyor sees McDonald's as the long-term market-share winner, he or she will be less than happy with a customer mix that emphasizes Wendy's and Burger King, or vice versa.

More Quality Measures: "I'll Know It When I See It!"

Supplier Mix

Does the organization have the right kind and right number of suppliers? There was a time when the more suppliers an organization had bidding for its business, the better. Now the prevailing policy is to have one or two excellent and well-integrated suppliers for each element. A ratio comparing numbers of suppliers to number of parts could be useful to the purchasing department and even the whole operations unit.

Employee Skill Mix

Although the employee skill mix might seem to be the province of the human resources department, it could become important for the whole company. If the strategic plan and its business plan identify business segments that will be more important to the future of the organization in, say, five years, the plan should go on to identify the critical needs associated with that shift in emphasis. That includes what kind of employees will be needed. Knowing now that the organization is overstocked with accountants and understocked with production planning specialists, for example, sets an obvious internal training objective for the next few years. In this situation, one approach would be to present the accountants with the option of being trained in advance for the production planning job. That way, the organization can retain good employees and its accountants can retain employment security.

Equipment Mix

If the business plan calls for proficiency in a certain machine or technology in five years, an organization should start it up now on a pilot basis or at a single location. Organizations that have been most successful in making the transition to flexible and just-in-time manufacturing conducted experiments well in advance—some of them relatively unsuccessful—as a learning vehicle that smoothed the subsequent mass transition. Equipment mix is also a critical measure in a fleet business, such as airlines or trucking, although the implicit philosophy may be very different from company to company. One may concentrate on reducing the number of vehicle types to streamline maintenance and improve efficiency; another may want to try every type available to hedge against going 100 percent in the wrong direction.

Geographic Mix

A globalizing company may want to calculate percent of value added per continent or trading block to see if it's truly globalizing fast enough. Along with value-added mix, it may also want to calculate national origin of management mix.

✿

Every type of business has it own vital mixes. The smart organization will do some mix research to see what kind of profile might be important to each of its families of measures.

SECTION IV

On the Front Line

Measurement can directly stimulate improvement by showing individual workers how things are progressing in their immediate work areas. But several indirect uses of measurement can stimulate major overall improvement.

The first is benchmarking. Performance measurement concentrates on continuous improvement, but the adequacy of the *level* of performance is also paramount. It's much easier to improve rapidly if you start off horribly than if you're in relatively good shape. Organizations that compare themselves with outside organizations can check their internal goal-setting and performance levels against an objective external standard. The most popular generic process benchmarking requires adherence to a disciplined but high-yield procedure. Not surprisingly, measurement is a vital part of describing the processes that are to be benchmarked. Unfortunately, although there are many types of and subjects for benchmarking, most organizations still are not using many of them.

Once an organization has used the benchmarking process to set realistic goals for itself, it must consider the needs of those who will help it achieve those goals—its employees. Many organizations turn to gainsharing, group incentive and involvement systems to reward workers for their improvement efforts. These plans are designed to allow the organization and its workforce to share measured gains. Most new plans are based on families of customized measures covering productivity, quality, customer satisfaction, and usually one or two other special concerns. The procedure to follow when planning, designing, and communicating a custom gainsharing plan is rigorous but highly rewarding—both for the individuals involved in the design process and for the overall organization.

Finally, organizations that are determined to make measurement an important part of their daily business routine will find that individual members of a family of measures can be aggregated using a unique matrix that effectively integrates improvement trends and improvement goals in one easy-to-follow display. Simplifying the tracking and attainment of goals will help the organization alter its measures when needed to reflect pressing new concerns and programs.

Just because an organization decides to embark on a measurement program doesn't mean that it will be a success. Measurement programs succeed—or fail—for many of the same reasons that other management interventions succeed or fail. But careful, thoughtful development of a comprehensive measurement system is one of the highest-yield projects that an organization can choose to undertake.

☼ 10 ☼

Benchmarking: "Are We There Yet?"

Organizations that measure performance are mainly concerned with improvement trends—that is, with knowing whether they're improving at a satisfactory pace. First, they spend a great deal of time determining what they want to improve and clearing away any technical difficulties that might cloud their reading of the improvement. Then the questions for the organization to ask become, "How much improvement do we want? As much as possible? As much as is cost-effective? As much as the president tells us to achieve? Enough to stay competitive?" All these questions can provide part of the answer, but goal-setting of this sort—based on carefully thought-out strategic planning initiatives—is a severely underrated art.

W. Edwards Deming pointed out the danger of goal-setting. When an organization reaches a particular goal, it tends to relax. Most organizational attempts at continuous improvement presume ongoing efforts toward perfection or zero-defects. The danger of the zero defects sort of goal is that it's easy for the members of an organization to become discouraged when they know that, despite public exhortations to the contrary, they will never reach their goal. So most organizations compromise. Moderately difficult goals are set. When they are reached, the organization celebrates, sets a new higher goal, and starts over again. But these intermediate goals are usually set quite arbitrarily using either a nice, absolute round-number target—such as 2,000 units per hour in the year 2000—or a simple improvement rate—such as a 6 percent improvement forever. These may turn out to be exactly the "right" targets that, once hit, will ensure that the organization achieves competitive balance, meets its earnings goals, or accomplishes its overriding objectives, but usually they aren't quite right.

Benchmarking, on the other hand, derives from the quality concept of management by fact.[1] Through it, an organization sets goals based on what it has seen other organizations do. If organization A can do something in a certain efficient or high-quality manner, so then, can organization B, given the appropriate time and resources. This sort of goal is neither so difficult to achieve as to be discouraging nor so easy to attain that it leads to underachievement.

Benchmarking Defined

Benchmarking can be defined as the systematic comparison of elements of the performance of an organization against that of other organizations, usually with the aim of mutual improvement.

Systematic means that the comparison is carefully planned, data are gathered and interpreted specifically for this purpose, and organized improvement of processes is the direct result of the exercise. The *elements* of performance that are to be compared will vary widely from organization to organization. Some are looking for the lightest product design, others want fastest cycle time, and still others want lowest cost along with the maintenance of specific features. Since there's no single definition of "best" practices, an organization that embarks on benchmarking must carefully define its goals. For example, it's not enough to say that the organization wants to become world-class in its field. There's no such thing as a world-class organization. There are world-class practices, processes, and approaches, but no organization is best or even good at all of them. There is undoubtedly a world-class focused marketer and another world-class broad-line marketer, but there can't be a single world-class marketer unless an organization can be both focused and broad-line at the same time.

Organization means any size or type of organization, ranging from a whole company or agency to a small work group. The most meaningful comparisons are often at the middle-level, functional sections of departments or key business processes that cut across an organization, such as customer complaint handling or community relations.

Mutual improvement excludes corporate espionage and much of market research from the definition of benchmarking. To get something, you give something. Although the term *competitive benchmarking* still survives, most benchmarking is done with similar but not directly competitive organizations so there can be effective cooperation. Thus, many of the most heavily benchmarked issues are at least partly generic across industry lines.

There are three major types of benchmarking. The oldest and most common is *internal benchmarking*, a comparison between divisions or locations of a single company or agency. These mutual-exchange meetings between counterparts from different parts of the company haven't always been systematic or even constructive. A great deal of staff time is often spent trying to show that the apparently better performance of the other division stems from some kind of temporary or special situation and, therefore, has no bearing on the other divisions. If the same amount of time were spent trying to learn from that division's superior performance, the whole company might be better off or at least know why it wasn't.

In the 1970s IBM developed a form of internal benchmarking called the Common Staffing Study, which compared plants or staff groups in different parts of the world.[2] The number of people doing a certain activity was ratioed to units of that activity accomplished. There were many reasons, valid and invalid, why the numbers varied. Although discussing the differences was occasionally frustrating, doing so helped IBM generate a lot of information about the organization's drivers.

Another form of benchmarking is the *industry study* or *industry survey*. These are usually conducted by trade associations, consultants who specialize in a particular industry, or quasi-governmental research organizations that want to give industrial policy guidance. The usual data-gathering vehicle is the survey, although focus groups and phone interviews are also used. The conclusions are presented as tendencies of industry segments or in disguised form when relating individual organization data. This is sometimes called *strategic benchmarking* because the issues deal with the ways different companies in the industry address strategic issues rather than with operational detail. Typical strategic benchmarking issues include

- Major equipment capacities, configurations, and problems,

- Personnel statistics and mixes,

- Customer satisfaction results,

- Maintenance practices and costs,

- Vertical integration and farming in and farming out,

- Internal quality data, and

- Environmental practices.

Since the information is coming from direct competitors, these types of issues can be assessed effectively only by a trusted or legally mandated intermediary. When used alone, this sort of benchmarking can be dangerous. Sometimes a whole industry is content to continue "old" practices as long as no one gains an "unfair" advantage. Incredibly, some countries that are accustomed to industrial policy guidance from their government discourage the introduction of new approaches, putting a higher value on fairness and protection than on progress and competitiveness.

There are two ways to handle the third type of benchmarking,

Benchmarking: "Are We There Yet?"

which is the *generic cross-industry study*. Under the first approach, consultants will organize studies on a particular topic and invite organizations from different industries that are thought to have an interest in that subject to join the study. Whereas an industry survey might have hundreds of participants who invest only a few hours each in filling out surveys and interpreting results, a cross-industry study is more likely to have five to fifteen participants who each invest several months—and substantial money—in developing the guidelines and parameters for the study; responding to various data-gathering approaches, including hosting consultant visits; and analyzing the results with and from the consultants.

The second cross-industry approach calls for an individual organization to systematically choose an organization or organizations with which to share detailed information one on one. For example, let's say that company A wants to study truck scheduling. After conducting a thorough analysis, it concludes that company B in another industry is the best truck scheduler. A asks B for help with truck scheduling and offers to help B in some area that B feels is lacking in its organization. On reflection, B chooses to hear about A's world-famous approach to supplier management, and a benchmarking relationship is born.

Which of these types of benchmarking is best? Most organizations should consider all of them. Large and disparate organizations can learn a great deal from internal benchmarking, but there's always the risk that they're too in-bred and none of their divisions is very good. Small companies have little ability to do much internal benchmarking since they typically handle one business in one location. Small and medium-size companies may get the most value from industry-based, strategic benchmarking, which is economical and a good first step in looking for strategic areas that would benefit from the closer inspection of small group or one-on-one benchmarking later. The success of the consultant-led cross-industry studies depend largely on the ability of the consultant to attract top-notch participants and extract from them nontrivial information without outrageous cost. The one-on-one cross-industry approach has the potential for providing detailed information at a reasonable cost for those willing to respect the discipline and thoroughness involved.

Benchmarking by Subject

Another way to divide types of benchmarking activity is by the type of data being compared rather than the manner in which the project is organized. Most benchmarking projects end up being mixed—that is, collecting several kinds of data. But they often start with a focus on one type.

Everyone is exposed to financial benchmarking. Business magazines fill their pages with comparisons of rates of growth, return on investment, earnings levels, and price trends of companies and mutual funds. As discussed in Chapter 4, these kinds of data are interesting, especially at the top of the organization, but it's not very useful in helping operating people make improvements of value in the workplace.

For many years organizations have analyzed the technical performance of their products through laboratory evaluations and other controlled testing experiences. Service delivery is often audited and compared in great detail by comparison shoppers. Market research surveys analyze and compare vital customers' perceptions of products and services. These are all forms of benchmarking. At the operational level, key practices and equipment are usually benchmarked in a binary mode (that is, with questions that require a yes or no response or a choice between two options)—for example, "Do you have X machinery? Do you farm out a certain type of processing? Do you use brokers or do you sell direct?"

Another interesting form of data that can be collected at the operational level is the process and department description developed in group and one-on-one format projects. Managers who traditionally considered benchmarking a form of numerical comparison making are finding that much can be learned from verbal descriptions and their graphic equivalent, flowcharts.

Of course, there are plenty of numerical comparisons that can be made at the operational level. Company A produces forty-two units an hour; company B produces only thirty-eight. But unless the conditions of such a comparison are strictly controlled, this kind of comparison is usually misleading. Direct comparisons can be made, however, between, say, two plants that have each just bought and installed an Acme 482 drill stand and use it to perforate the same type of metal. In fact, most of the effort in all forms of benchmarking goes into searching for controlled conditions so that relevant comparisons like this can be made.

One-on-One Benchmarking

Benchmarking is a detailed discipline composed of several critical steps. Although some of the steps outlined below can be reordered and, in some cases, even skipped, an organization would be wise to follow each of these steps during its first attempts at benchmarking.

1. Choose the Topic

The main source of benchmarking topics is typically executive intuition that manifests itself directly (as in the statement "I think we need to do better in X") or indirectly (as in "The strategic plan calls for more attention to X"). This intuition can be based on years of valid experience and observation, a business magazine article, or a conversation during a golf game.

2. Choose the Benchmarking Team

The quality of the team selection process will ultimately make or break the benchmarking effort. Emphasizing a team effort eliminates the notion of an individual benchmarking expert. Just as there is no world-class-in-everything company, so there's no such person as an all-around benchmarking expert. Benchmarking requires a wide range of experiences and skills that no one individual can possess.

The team should be a diagonal slice of the organization, with representatives from all relevant functions with interest in the topic and from several layers of the organization. The project sponsor has to rank high enough to protect the team from organizational road-blocks and resource shortages. The team should include some "doers" who know the way things are actually done regarding the selected topic and can help smooth the way when the better system is ready to be installed. The "process owner" or his or her representative needs to be involved, too.

Composed of eight to ten members, the ideal team boasts such skills as meeting facilitation, technical process expertise, accounting system mastery, writing and presenting, and flowcharting. Someone must know about the final customers' needs. Training will be needed to fill any skill gaps, especially in conducting meetings and flowcharting.

3. Gather External Data

Once the benchmarking team has carefully defined the boundaries of the project and received its training, it will often split into outside and inside subteams. The outside team will find out what information about the topic is in the public domain. There's usually more than expected. Organizations like to brag about their excellent performance, and there's no shortage of journalists looking for a story. Trade associations, consultants, bankers, former employees, and even neighbors might have threads of information that, when combined, form a clear picture of who does that topic activity well—or thinks they do.

4. Gather Internal Data

Meanwhile, the other subteam is gathering information about the different ways the topic is handled in the various parts of the organization. The "doers" are interviewed, and their testimony is compared with the organization's procedures manual or equivalent. It's important to note that organizational procedures manuals tend to be outdated and may not even recognize the existence of some of the newer cross-cutting processes because they're not "managed" by any recognized department chief. The information to be gathered includes at least the following:

○ Definition and boundaries of the process,

○ Inputs to the process,

○ Outputs from the process,

○ Process owner and participants identification,

○ Measures of the process,

○ Inspections and reviews conducted,

○ Improvements already underway,

○ Subprocess identification, and

○ Previous benchmarks used.

5. Select a Partner

The subteams reunite and share their findings. Now they know what the organization does, what they're looking for, and something about who out there is doing well. The sponsor or orginating executives may also have partners in mind, dating back to the original conversation on the golf course or magazine article they read. There are also clearinghouses that have been developed to help in this process.

It's presumptuous for an organization to assume that everyone wants to benchmark with it; it needs to have something to offer. If the ideal partner also happens to be a supplier or customer, that might be sufficient; they want the organization to do well and should be willing to help. But in the absence of a special connection, the organization initiating the benchmarking effort has to offer some useful reciprocal help.

6. Organize Field Benchmarking

Once the partner is signed up, a team from each organization must meet to set up ground rules on confidentiality, priorities, and timing. It's unlikely that the new partner will be immediately prepared with the same depth of information that the initiating partner has developed, although it should understand the topics being studied and have plenty of documentation. Also, the organization initiating the benchmarking relationship has to prepare information on the topic that it is going to help its partner with.

7. Conduct Field Benchmarking

Once all the preparation on both sides has been done, the two teams should meet and compare flowcharts and measurement data. Each should politely challenge the other's reasons for doing things the way they do them so that understanding is clear. Site visits will typically be exchanged so the processes can be seen in action, even though some are entirely handled with computers, rendering the site visit largely symbolic. A major reason for the failure of benchmarking is that site visits are done too early in the benchmarking sequence and team members aren't sure what they're looking for.

8. Implement the Improvement

When the benchmarking team returns home and analyzes the data it collected, it may conclude that there's no reason to change the current system. But there are usually some better practices to be installed and sometimes the conclusion of the project is, in effect, "Let's blow up the old system and start over." The benchmarking team, or at least some of the local members, usually takes the lead in proposing, defending, and ultimately installing the new system.

9. Seed the Next Round

The benchmarking team members will be helpful in training the next benchmarking team. Frequently some of the original participants are asked to be permanent benchmarking leaders and may direct other projects and implementations. The next round may be conducted with the same partner and new topics, or it may find an appropriate new partner or partners. Sometimes, especially in MIS applications, the newly installed system may need to be expanded to include suppliers, customers, distributors, or franchisees.

The Relationship Between
Benchmarking and Measurement

Most benchmarkers do benchmarking to make major performance improvements—breakthroughs instead of mere continuous improvement. It's hard to criticize the search for major improvement, but even minor improvement is worth having. Good benchmarking work can help an organization dedicate its resources to high-potential projects.

Even before making external comparisons, the benchmarking teams can gain substantial value in simply seeing how a process is accomplished in different parts of their own organization. Drawing a flowchart of a current complex reality will sometimes highlight the redundancy and unnecessary complication of the "official" way of doing business, and improvements can be made without ever going outside the organization. Moreover, those concerned with employee development will appreciate the value of a benchmarking team experience in teaching employees how an organization works.

Clearly performance measurement and benchmarking overlap a great deal. A measurement system that concentrates only on performance trends fails to differentiate between relative easy improvement (from horrible to fair) and relatively difficult improvement (from good to excellent). This failure will discourage managers from taking on the important improvement tasks of the organization. Benchmarking is the major technique for generating meaningful level-of-performance information so that an organization can rationally set goals.

There is also a key role for measurement data in benchmarking projects. Once the systems to be compared are understood enough so that similarities and differences can be clearly recognized, the various performance measures help determine which is the better system regarding the variable being compared (cost, time, quality). The hard part is convincing busy managers to have the patience to delay any numerical comparisons until the similarities and differences can be understood.

☼ 11 ☼

Gainsharing: "What's in It for Me?"

As an organization begins to listen to its customers, take strategic plans seriously, and use performance measures to guide improvement efforts throughout the organization, the employees who do all this begin to think of themselves as the responsible parties. "The formal organization provided the resources, but, we, the employees, are the difference between how things used to be and how they are now," they reason. "We get to keep our jobs—no small thing in the current climate—but what difference does it make if we give the solid, regular effort or a little extra effort or few extra minutes that nobody will notice? We'll get the same wages, same promotion prospects, and same job security, but less time at home."

Organizations eager to encourage employee commitment are looking for a way to generate additional interest in and enthusiasm for improving operating results. Gainsharing provides this additional spark without "costing" the company anything.[1] It can convert technically good but apathetic workers—including middle management, supervisors, and operating and support employees— into improvement zealots. The typical plan is mostly self-managed by the workforce as a whole, and it often provides an invaluable focal point for an empowered organization.

Gainsharing is a group-incentive and involvement system. The gain, calculated according to a predetermined formula, represents improvement that the organization wouldn't otherwise have accomplished. Shared between the owners of the organization and the employees in the relevant units on a current (within a year) basis, the gain is the ultimate answer to the question, "What's in it for me?"

Although historically there have been many approaches to gainsharing, the main focus discussed here is on a system based on the family-of-measures approach to measurement. The approach includes careful planning that follows a readiness assessment, design by a group of employees, thorough communications, and a carefully derived and strategy-linked formula.

Traditional Gainsharing Plans

The Scanlon plan was developed in the mid–1930s when a union official named Joe Scanlon, on behalf of his members, proposed that the workforce would help management find better ways of working to keep their failing company solvent. The first innovation was an employee suggestion system, which was very successful. A monetary bonus feature was added several years later when the company had recovered from the Depression.

The Scanlon formula is based on labor cost as a percentage of output value, as variously defined. Thus, for example, if payroll as a percentage of sales starts off with a base of 28 percent, reducing that to 24 percent would result in the labor force and the owner splitting the 4 percent differential, usually 50–50 (see Table 11.1).

The Scanlon plan has been successful because it introduces employee involvement in a positive way. But its critics say that its simple payout formula is flawed because it doesn't take a number of critical factors into consideration. Price inflation in sales does not necessarily match wage inflation. The plan's payout has moved up and down based on both uncontrollable price movements and real

Gainsharing: "What's in It for Me?"

TABLE 11.1. EXAMPLE OF A SCANLON PLAN

Scanlon Plan Calculation	Base Period	Current Period
Sales	$1,000,000	$1,200,000
Payroll	$ 280,000	$ 288,000
Payroll at base of 28 percent	$ 280,000	$ 336,000
"Gain"	—	$ 48,000
"Gain" for workforce (50 percent)	—	$ 24,000
"Gain" per current payroll	—	8.3%
Bonus for worker making $1,500 per month	—	$125

productivity improvement. Much productivity improvement is driven by capital investment and automation, but in this scenario the owners have to pay for the whole investment but get only half of the improvement to apply against the amortization of the investment. Moreover, under this plan, workers had to face the reality that as long as production levels were maintained, the more of their colleagues who were laid off, the higher the bonuses.

Over time, other variations were developed. The Rucker plan used a value-added-to-payroll formula that recognized improvements in materials and energy. Multifactor Scanlon plans (payroll plus materials, for example) were also developed. The ultimate extension of multifactor Scanlon plans is a form of profit sharing—sales compared to all controllable costs.

All those plans are subject to the problem of incorporating inflation. Improshare uses a physical labor productivity formula—earned hours against standard hours of labor. Although this excludes direct attention to materials, capital, and energy, in some labor-intensive businesses those three inputs move roughly in proportion to direct labor. But what about quality, timeliness, safety, and so on?

Finally, traditional profit sharing has much in common with gainsharing, except that the payout is typically delayed until retirement or other departure from the company. This doesn't encourage the type of excitement that results from immediate recognition of current success. The profit calculation is typically made for the whole organization, thus making it difficult for the local worker to see his or her direct impact. Gainsharing is typically installed at the plant or division level, much closer to the worker's interest and understanding.

Gainsharing now almost entirely uses a custom formula—a family of four to six measures incorporating mostly if not exclusively physical measures of productivity, quality, timeliness, safety, and other local interests. Although gainsharing plans tend to be classified by formula, there's also some variety in the involvement system. Suggestion systems are still found, but the involvement efforts are now often linked with quality teams administered through an organizationwide continuous improvement effort. The teams take the lead in working toward planned improvement in quality, but the whole relevant organization benefits from the improvement in the performance indicators without regard to who was on the teams.

Gainsharing Planning Issues

There are four main issues to consider when planning a gainsharing program.

Readiness

The most important planning issue is whether the organization is ready for such a venture. When the idea is first considered, there are always some at the top of the organization who feel, "We already pay good salaries for full performance; that should be enough." Of course, they are usually part of the executive bonus plan that pays performance bonuses on top of a good salary, but somehow that's different. The organization must have confidence in its workforce and be willing to provide tools, training, and rewards without hassle.

There is also a timing issue. It's better to install a gainsharing plan as the business cycle is on the upswing rather than heading downward. Although formula elements can be devised that are quite sheltered from the business cycle, there's bound to be some impact. It's important that gainsharing pay out a reasonable amount the first few periods, or it may never take off.

Boundaries

Gainsharing is normally installed in a single-location plant or office location with everyone (or nearly everyone) included in the plan. Wherever there is an interdependent, multiple-location "circuit," these can all be part of the same plan. But if all the multiple plants share, for example, the same group executive, they should have separate plans for each location.

Successful gainsharing plans cover from about 50 to 800 workers. Organizations with fewer than 50 workers are probably better off with a current-pay profit-sharing plan, which is easier to install and explain. In organizations with more than 800 workers, the connection between what an employee does and what he or she receives is stretched. In this case, dividing the group into two or three subgroups, each with its own plan, should be considered. It's possible to have layered plans where everyone is part of a plan dealing with the 300-person work group but is also part of a plan for the entire 1,200-person plant. This hedges against great performance in some areas going unrewarded because of poor performance elsewhere, but it also introduces more complexity and intergroup jealousy and transfer pressure.

Union Participation

If there's a union, it would be much better to introduce a jointly designed plan rather than impose a management-directed one, regardless of how enlightened the imposed plan appears to be. Imposed plans sometimes have worked well and have gained after-the-fact acceptance by unions that were initially uninterested in them. In practice, the local unionized workers are normally interested in the gainsharing idea, but sometimes senior labor leaders see it as eroding the union's reason for being. However, the most successful plans are those where the local union leaders participate on the design team and help with communication and administration from the beginning.

Design Team

The ideal design team for gainsharing sounds a great deal like the ideal benchmarking team described in Chapter 10. This is not a surprise, since the required work and insight are similar. A diagonal slice of the organization to be covered is appropriate, including members from management, union ("floor") workers, and nonunion, nonmanagement office workers. Skills needed include meeting facilitation and planning, technical process familiarity, accounting, and human resources knowledge. The team of eight to ten individuals should be available to meet every week for at least two to four hours.

Gainsharing Design Issues

When designing a gainsharing plan, an organization must consider five major points.

Eligibility

Once the boundaries are set, details concerning inclusions have to be worked out. Typically a person has to work a certain minimum amount of time in each bonus period to receive a full share of the gains. "Work" may or may not include days off, vacations, sick leave, jury duty, and so on. It's often specified that workers must be on the payroll at both the beginning and the end of the period, so as to exclude very new and probationary workers at the front end and turning-over or retiring workers at the other end. The impact of part-time and temporary workers needs to be analyzed also.

Medium of Payment

Medium of payment is easy—cash! But there are a few plans that offer merchandise catalog or airline travel points instead. The argument is that the purchasing power of the company allows it to cut discount deals on merchandise and travel, and these rewards are more memorable over the long term than undifferentiated cash awards. But there is risk in trying to be a social engineer in an environment where cash is known to be acceptable to everyone.

Frequency of Payout

Although the frequency of payout can range from weekly to annually, most plans pay out rewards either monthly or quarterly. Frequent payments serve to remind everyone about the existence of the plan, but they're relatively small and will tend to be spent as part of the individual's family routine. Less frequent payments will be relatively larger and may go for larger, more memorable items. The "reminding" function can be served by reporting data monthly but cutting checks quarterly.

Split

The normal practice in the United States is that everyone receives the same percent bonus. The employees' share of the gain is divided by the eligible payroll to arrive at the bonus percent. This means that management participants tend to get substantially more absolute dollars than the "floor" workers, which contradicts the message of teamwork and cooperation that the organization is ostensibly trying to send. Organizations outside the United States typically give the same absolute amount to everyone, a much more defensible approach. Those considering this option, however, have to bear in mind that U.S. labor law appears to force recalculation of the overtime rate if the same-absolute-amount approach is used. Organizations that don't have a lot of overtime to calculate will be unperturbed; but those with more overtime will probably want to stick with the former approach.

Share

There's a certain "American-way" appeal to the concept of sharing the gain 50–50 between the company and the workforce. But that feeling should be resisted in the early design phases, in spite of the Scanlon and Improshare (discussed above) precedents in that direction. The share will ultimately need to take into account what measures are selected for the formula and how "rich" they are in terms of improvement potential. For example, note the difference between A and B in Table 11.2.

In 1987, the median gainsharing plan that paid anything paid about 8 percent of payroll. Less than, say, 3 percent in a good year would generally be considered tokenism or worse. More than 12 to 15 percent would be consided by most owners as overkill. If there are five different measures in the family, there are five different

TABLE 11.2. TWO GAINSHARING PLANS

	Company A	Company B
Sales	$1,000,000	$1,000,000
Materials cost	$ 400,000	$ 400,000
Estimated yield improvement potential in first year	$ 20,000	$ 20,000
Payroll	$ 400,000	$ 100,000
Relation of 50 percent of yield gain to payroll	2.5%	10%
Share of gain required to give 2 percent of payroll	40%	10%

ways for the workforce to earn money. But the five combined have to offer enough potential so that, after being shared, the payout approximately arrives at the organization's target percent of payroll.

Communicating the Gainsharing Plan

There are four points to consider when communicating a gain-sharing plan.

The Design Phase

The design team should be keeping its various constituencies informed during the design process and soliciting opinions by direct discussion or even by survey on the issues as they come up. In some cases, volunteers might be brought in for special subteam assignments. The more the plan is perceived as the work of a great many of the organization's employees, the easier it will be to launch and the more effective it will be in the long run.

Involvement Linkages

If there are preexisting involvement efforts, these teams or forums should be prepared to cooperate with and even feature the issues identified for concentration by the gainsharing formula. It's certainly not appropriate to have competing gainsharing teams and quality teams or individual-reward suggestion systems. If there's a quality council, it should be represented or even be dominant on the gainsharing design team so as to ensure the integration of the organization's involvement effort.

Individual Motivation

Thought should be given to the individual motivational techniques used in the organization and how they would fit with gainsharing.

It's possible to be both a good team player and an individual star, but those who want to do only "their share" need to be accommodated, too. Individual merit pay systems are usually not that at all but rather an inflation-adjustment machine run wild. True merit recognition, by definition, covers only unusual performance by, say, 10 to 15 percent of the workforce.

Pay-for-knowledge or skill-pay systems fit well with gainsharing. They reward individuals for becoming certified in other formal skills or trades even if they aren't doing that type of work at present. This provides flexibility of assignment and individual stimulation for the more ambitious of the workforce, without disrupting group arrangements.

Launch Phase and Later Administration

Great attention needs to be given to the launch of the plan. If there has been good communication with the workforce during design, there will be better understanding of the details. But understanding is not enough. As in marketing a new product, the "customers" (in this case, the workforce) must positively want to get into this new thing called "gains." All media are needed—booklets and brochures for the older folks and videos and bands for the young.

Frequently, after the plan is launched the design team is resurrected as the administration team with a provision for gradual turnover in, say, the next three years. The design team members are most interested in the plan's success and are most knowledgeable about it, so it would be foolish to replace them with amateurs from either management or the union. The administration team calculates and publishes results as they occur, resolves eligibility questions, and perhaps every year reviews the measures and modifies them if warranted.

Arriving at a Gainsharing Formula

There are six factors to consider when creating a gainsharing formula.

The Organization's Family of Measures

There's little that's special about selecting measures for the gainsharing plan. Ideally, the organization will already have families of measures everywhere, including at the top of the organization where the decision to gainshare was made. Then it's strongly advised to use those same measures. If some of the existing measures are not suitable for either political or technical reasons, others can be selected. Political reasons include worker aversion to labor productivity as a payment mechanism for "bribing me to sacrifice my buddies." Technical reasons include immaturity (as in much customer-satisfaction surveying) or insufficient frequency or accuracy to be the basis for paying real money.

Baseline

Gain calculation requires two data points: how things were and how they are now. The setting of the calculation base is easy to state; choose a reflection of "normal." But people will differ on whether normal is the last three months, the last year, an average of the last three years, or even the new budget basis for next year.

Once the plan is started, should the base be ratcheted up each year or frozen at starting-point levels? A major reason for low employer satisfaction with some of the traditional plans is that they typically froze the base. Employees benefitted from the innovations of their fathers, and companies had to "buy out" plans to everyone's dissatisfaction. But a "full ratchet" may be unfair also. If an improvement innovation is installed in December, the workforce may receive only one month of reward from it before it's ratcheted away.

Thus, some organizations will do partial ratchets each year the base is adjusted—say, halfway between the past year's base and the actual level in practice at the end of that year.

Capital

If there's a measure of labor productivity in the family of measures, some provision may be needed to adjust for automation or other capital investment that led to an automatic improvement in labor productivity. The Improshare formula uses an 80–20 rule: the baseline is moved up 80 percent of the expected improvement amount, leaving 20 percent to be harvested by the workers as soon as they successfully install and learn to operate the new equipment efficiently.

The same philosophy can be applied to other "automatic" improvements where workforce thinking or innovation is peripheral. If a supplier volunteers a new size of raw material sheet that reduces design scrap, that savings may not be included in scrap gain. But if the organization's own employees suggest that to the supplier, and it wouldn't have happened without that push, the gain should be in the plan calculation.

Valuation and Aggregation

Valuation refers to the translation of physical gains into dollar terms. Aggregation is the combination of the several separate gains into one total. If the family of measures is expressed in binary terms, the valuation is quite general and the aggregation is trivial. *Binary* means a target is set for each measure that's either attained or not, and an amount of money is either earned for the gain pool or not. For example, based on the data provided in Table 11.3, every employee would get $600. They hit three targets and missed three. There is some sense in the valuation that some of the targets (those that have more dollars of reward attached) are more important than some of the others. Aggregation is by simple addition.

TABLE 11.3. EXAMPLE OF VALUATION AND AGGREGATION

Measure	Target Performance	Potential Bonus per Person	Actual Performance	Goal Reached?	Final Bonus per Person
Labor productivity	2,400 units	$300	2,380 units	No	0
Error rate of zzz	3.0%	$250	2.7%	Yes	$250
Cycle time of xxx	15 days	$200	14.9 days	Yes	$200
Safety (number of reportable incidents)	3	$150	6	No	0
Customer satisfaction index	90%	$150	85%	No	0
Environmental index	80%	$150	84%	Yes	$150
Total bonus paid to each person					$600

In a continuous-function case the situation is quite different and more complicated because there is an infinite amount of potential outcomes. Many feel that the continuous-function case is worth the extra work because the binary approach is plagued by the problem Deming identified regarding the attainment of goals: once an organization reaches a goal, it tends to relax for a while. Continuous improvement does not permit relaxing, and the continuous function simply allows more and more gain to translate indirectly into more and more reward. A continuous function example is provided in Table 11.4. The share is 40–60 and there are seventy employees, so the average bonus is $58,500 × .40 = $23,400/70 = $334 per employee.

The valuation is relatively easy for labor productivity, since there's a direct connection between labor hours and dollars. It's quite arbitrary for the other measures, since there's little commonality among

TABLE 11.4. A CONTINUOUS FUNCTION EXAMPLE

Measure	Base Performance	New Performance	Absolute Improve- ment	Bonus per Unit of Improve- ment	Total Gain to be Shared
Labor productivity	2,340 units	2,380 units	40 units	$ 500	$20,000
Error rate	3.2%	2.7%	0.5%	$40,000	$20,000
Cycle time	17 days	14.9 days	2.1 days	$15,000	$31,500
Safety (number of reportable incidents)	5	6	(1)	$10,000	($10,000)
Customer satisfaction index	88%	85%	(3)	$10,000	($30,000)
Environmental index	75%	84%	9%	$ 3,000	$27,000
Total gains to be shared					$58,500

the different types of errors and the other measures are simple approximations. Yet another approach uses continuous functions and an objectives matrix (see Chapter 12).

Caps and Gates

Sometimes one or more of the formula elements are subject to partly uncontrollable fluctuation. For example, an organization that wants to call everyone's attention to energy conservation chooses energy productivity as a member of its family of measures. But energy use is partly influenced by weather conditions. So if the organization says no more than X can be earned and no more than Y can be lost with the energy component of the formula, it ensures fairness in the calculation while keeping energy uppermost in people's minds.

Gainsharing: "What's in It for Me?"

Sometimes an organization's owners have an overriding concern, usually "profits," in the absence of which they don't want to make a gainsharing payment. This is a gate. As long as profits are made according to a certain formula, gains are generated and share arrangements hold. But if the profits fall below zero, the plan is suspended or the share percentage shifts downward until the organization's health improves. Thus, a plan that normally features a 40–60 share might switch to a 20–80 while the organization is suffering a loss.

Gates are also sometimes installed for quality or safety reasons. But they are motivationally disturbing; all it takes is one or two gate "applications" and the value of the plan is ruined. It's considered unfair if local workers make massive improvements but see their efforts blown away by incompetence in another part of the organization. But a gainsharing plan with gates is certainly better than no gainsharing plan at all.

Reserves

It's common to have a one-year cycle on a plan but to pay out gains quarterly or monthly. This means there's a chance of premature payout that cannot be recaptured from the workforce. If great gains and payouts are made early in the cycle but all the improvement ground is lost later in the cycle, the company is compromised. So reserves of 20 to 25 percent of gain payout to the workforce are created to serve as a cushion, if needed. If not needed, these are paid out at the end of the year.

The Value and Limitations of Gainsharing

Gainsharing has some great advantages but cannot solve all of an organization's problems. Disparities in base salaries, either between labor and management within the organization or between a gainsharing organization and other local employers, will not be solved by normal gainsharing plans. A few organizations, such as Nucor Steel, have developed massive gainsharing plans to bridge between a very low prevailing wage rate in the locality but a very high rate within the industry, but that is an exception. Also, as mentioned earlier, gainsharing needs to be integrated with the individual incentive policy to keep highly motivated individuals content. And it has to be installed at an appropriate time in the organization's business cycle.

When done well, gainsharing can fill a very important gap in providing clear incentive and motivation in the middle and bottom of the organization comparable to the executive bonuses at the top. And it can be done in such a way that reaps gains for the company that it would otherwise not have received. For those interested in developing respect for a comprehensive performance measurement system, this better than any other means puts the measurement system on center stage and allows management by fact to become the primary way of doing business throughout the organization.[2]

☼ **12** ☼

Ready, Set, Measure

Now, go out and develop a measurement system! The philosophy and approach for doing so should be clear. But what kind of day-to-day techniques are needed to simplify the process? We know why we're measuring and we know what to measure; now let's figure out where to measure and how.

Where is fairly easy to determine—wherever someone wants to measure something. Although it makes more theoretical sense to roll out a measurement-development process in the same manner as a strategic plan, many organizations have real problems mobilizing such an impressive effort, given all the other things that need to be done and the normal shortage of willing volunteers for any new activity, however meritorious. Therefore, many organizations start measuring on a pilot basis, choosing a few willing volunteer departments or sections and letting them go through the development procedure themselves, either alone or with a consultant. Organizations that have no trouble drumming up volunteers are often among the best managed, so the odds of their producing good results are high. Once a few pilots have finished developing their own measurement systems and made presentations about them to the rest of the organization, it should be clear that mere mortals can, indeed, successfully develop measures in a relatively short period of time, provided that the unit's planning basis is sound and its local management supportive.

How to Measure

How to measure is a more complicated issue. Many managers have tried what they think is benchmarking. They call up some friends, find out what they measure, and then do the same. This is *not* the proper way to benchmark. Each organization is different and needs the customized attention of its own people, both to get the "right" measures in the first place and to ensure that they are respected and used to stimulate improvement throughout the organization. Transplanting a set of measures, regardless of the pedigree of its source, won't accomplish either goal. To make the measurement process as painless—and effective—and possible, there are a number of things organizations can do.

Use the nominal group technique to help reach a consensus on tough issues.

Nominal group technique (NGT) is a structured brainstorming approach that's useful for resolving any open-ended question where there may be strong differences in opinion and preference among the members of a group that needs to reach a consensus.[1] *Nominal* refers to the fact that the group using the technique is a group in name only. Made up of eight to ten people, it looks like a group, but the approach used to achieve consensus starts off very protective of individual opinions. It takes the group three to four hours to come to an unpolished consensus that one or two members of the group can go on and convert into a finished recommendation. Here's the basic approach:

Step 1 The topic is selected; in this case, "What measures of performance should be used by the ABC department?"

Step 2 A diagonal-slice group is selected, once again much like the groups chosen in Chapter 10, which discussed benchmarking, and Chapter 11, which focused on gainsharing. It should contain members of the ABC department from different ranks, a customer or two of the ABC department, perhaps someone who oversees the department from above or an alumnus, and, since the topic at hand concerns measurement, someone who knows the accounting system well.

Step 3 A facilitator calls a one-day meeting of the group with little or no further explanation. The members gather and the facilitator defines the task and ground rules:

○ The task is to nominate a family of performance measures.

○ The measures should be consistent with the latest strategic objectives (which should be clearly posted for easy reference).

○ Each participant is to give his or her own ideas without challenge from others. No cross-talk is allowed until the members are released from this discipline later in the meeting.

Step 4 For about ten minutes, the group members silently and independently think of ideas for measures and write them down.

Step 5 The facilitator leads a round robin in which everyone in turn nominates a measure idea, which the facilitator writes on a flip chart without comment. The round robin continues until ideas stop flowing. A participant can pass on his or her turn and jump back in the next time around. The participants are encouraged to build on other participants' ideas. The typical session will go five or six rounds, but it can still be going strong after ten or twelve rounds.

Step 6 An editing session is held in which each proposed measure is reviewed in two ways:

○ Is it redundant with other nominations on the list? If so, they are combined.

○ Is it understood by all? If not, the nominator is asked to explain.

No judgment is made on the importance or usefulness of the ideas. Normally 15 to 20 percent of the nominations are eliminated through editing.

Step 7 Each participant votes by secret ballot for a designated number of the nominated ideas. There are many ways of doing this. One way is to have each person vote for the eight best measures, with eight points for the best, seven for the next best, and so on, to one point for the eighth best. Votes are added, and the top ten finishers are displayed.

Step 8 Participants are free to explain their nominations and votes and criticize the draft consensus reached by the ten winners. There will be less animosity than might be expected, for although participants may have entered the room with very different ideas, the brainstorming process tends to homogenize opinion substantially. Who proposed what tends to be forgotten, and the team members start working together to determine whether the top five or six measures are well balanced or whether some of the seventh- through tenth-place finishers need to be brought in as substitutes to ensure better overall balance.

Step 9 Usually one or two of the group members agree to work with the facilitator to further refine the consensus and present it to the approval executive, who was not a participant in the NGT meeting.

NGT is an effective and inexpensive way to develop measures participatively. Those who work in small departments or with individual processes may not need to use the NGT. The few members of the group can sit down and brainstorm. But NGT allows a relatively small proportion of a large group to do a good job of providing measures for the whole group.

Set a clear and accurate baseline.

As discussed in Chapter 11, demonstrating improvement requires two pieces of data: how things used to be and how they are now. When organizations try to set a baseline—how things used to be— they often are faced with a wide array of "past periods" that could be used. The overall goal is to identify the best indicator of normal times to avoid the influence of special conditions, but opinions on that subject will certainly differ.

The safest strategy is to present a great deal of data in graphical form and let each person draw his or her own conclusion. Whether a process variable plotted in a particular figure is "getting better" or not sometimes depends on what you want the answer to be. With further discussion, a consensus can be reached so that no one can later claim to have been mislead.

Integrate improvement trends and goals through aggregation.

Each of the individual members of a family of measures has its own identity and trends and, therefore, can be analyzed separately. The measures can also be looked at as five or six separate measures viewed together, and some overall judgment can be rendered on "net" progress. But that generally isn't good enough for everyone— and it shouldn't be. It's not difficult to objectively aggregate a family of measures to provide a single improvement rate number. There are two ways to do this: by simple aggregation and by using the objectives matrix.

The only advantage of simple aggregation—that it is simple—is not a trivial one. Table 12.1 provides an example of how it works. The 1.039 total means that peformance of the overall family of measures shown here improved a weighted average of 3.9 percent, with major gains in error rate, cycle time, and environmental index and a minor gain in labor productivity partly offset by a small decline in customer satisfaction and a major decline in safety.

What's missing from this analysis is the answer to the question,

TABLE 12.1. AN EXAMPLE OF SIMPLE AGGREGATION

Measure	Base Data	Current Data	Improve- ment	Weight	Weighte Improv ment
Labor productivity	2,340 units	2,380 units	1.017	.25	.254
Error rate	3.2%	2.7%	1.156	.20	.231
Cycle time	17.0 days	14.9 days	1.124	.15	.169
Safety (number of reportable incidents)	5.0	6.0	.800	.10	.080
Customer satisfaction index	88%	85%	.966	.20	.193
Environmental index	75%	84%	1.120	.10	.112
Total weighted improvement:					1.039

"What was expected to happen in this period?" There's no indication of goals. The cycle-time gain looks big, unless the goal is to go from seventeen days to five days this year. Then progress to 14.9 days isn't so good after all. The decline in customer satisfaction—which is presented on the table as .966 and means the same as 3.4 percent—appears small, but when an organization already starts with an 88 percent satisfaction rate, major improvement will require getting very near the 100 percent mark. A decline of 3 percent instead of an increase approaching 12 percent may be a disaster. In short, a percentage increase in a number doesn't say much about what the final number should be. That's the main reason that this simple method of measuring progress is too simple for most organizations.

A better approach involves using the objectives matrix, also known as the Oregon matrix because it was developed at Oregon State University in the 1980s.[2] In this technique, a little extra complexity is more than offset by the ability to include prevailing goals and reflect intermediate progress toward them in a way that everyone will understand.

Figure 12.1 presents a completed objectives matrix. Much of the information is the same as that shown in Table 12.1. The names of

Ready, Set, Measure

FIGURE 12.1. A SAMPLE OBJECTIVES MATRIX

Labor Productivity	Error Rate	Cycle Time	Safety	Customer Satisfaction	Environment Index	
2,380	2.70	14.9	6.0	85	84	Actual Performance
2,700	2.00	5.0	2.0	95	90	•• 10
2,650	2.15	6.5	2.3	94	88	••• 9
2,600	2.30	8.0	2.6	93	86	••• 8
2,550	2.45	9.5	3.0	92	(84)	••• 7
2,500	2.60	11.0	3.5	91	82	••• 6
2,450	(2.80)	13.0	4.0	90	80	••• 5
2,400	3.00	(15.0)	4.5	89	78	••• 4
(2,340)	3.20	17.0	5.0	88	75	••• 3
2,300	3.45	19.0	5.6	87	72	••• 2
2,250	3.70	21.5	(6.3)	86	68	••• 1
2,200	4.00	24.0	7.0	(85)	64	••• 0
25	20	15	10	20	10	Weight
3.7	5.5	4.1	1.4	0	7.0	Score
93	110	62	14	0	70	Value TOTAL 349

the measures (located at the top of each column), their respective base (row 3), and actual performance data are the same, as are the weights. The only new data—the goals for a time period in the future—are given in row 10. This is how to use the objectives matrix:

1. Develop an appropriately balanced family of four to six measures for the process or department to be measured.

2. On the empty matrix, list those measures as column heads and develop an appropriate weighting system to insert in the weight row. The weights should add up to 100.

3. Calculate or otherwise assume a base value for each measure and insert those values in row 3.

4. Develop a goal for each measure for a time in the future—say, three years out—and insert that in row 10. The amount of effort—or stretch—required to go from row 3 to row 10 should be roughly comparable for each of the measures.

5. Fill in values for rows 4 through 9 and 0 through 2 in each column. There are three common ways of doing this:

   ✿ Apply the same absolute value for each step.

   ✿ Apply the same percentage improvement for each step.

   ✿ If it is a measure where "the going gets tougher as you get better," apply increasingly small steps as you approach row 10.

6. Now the grid is ready for measuring. Let a full period pass and calculate actual results for each measure. Insert the results in the actual-performance row and circle the score for each result where it appears in its column. Going from the circle to the 0 to 10 scale at the right, record the corresponding number (or typically a decimal interpolation) in the score row.

7. Multiply the score in each column by the weight, putting the

product in the value row. Add the value row across and enter the sum in the total box in the bottom right corner. That number is the final score for this period. If it is better than 300, overall progress has been made.

8. Create a cluster of histograms going from the circle markings in each column downward. Share these results with the relevant workers and formulate new or corrected improvement plans.

9. As time passes and most column scores approach or exceed 10, have a grand celebration and start over with a new matrix and still more ambitious goals.

The objectives matrix provides a full report on one piece of paper or one computer screen on how the organization has done in relation to its base and its goals in the last period, both for individual measures and the family as a whole. If each family of measures throughout the organization uses the same format, anyone can immediately understand and help analyze the situation in another group. As with most measurement, it identifies where the problem appears but not necessarily what caused it. Nonetheless, it is a starting point for identifying the root causes of organizational problems.

Plan an effective feedback system.

Any comprehensive measurement system should provide all the kinds of feedback required. Regardless of the type of feedback—whether to work groups for self-correction or to supervisors for obtaining revised orders—it's an advantage to have decided what is of most importance and to routinely calculate and graph progress in a consistent format.

Routinely providing measured results is always better than issuing data on demand or only on a need-to-know basis. As systems become more complex and everyone has a higher degree of responsibility and analytical expectation, knowing that the data are always available lets individuals test ideas as needed rather than filing them away to form a new project to be studied when the data ultimately do arrive. It also takes away the compulsion to "do something" every time some new data appear. Individuals and groups will become used to tracking data over time and proposing improvement action or experimentation only when a clear pattern emerges.

Although the phrase *open organization* is usually thought of in regard to progressive human resources policies, voluntarily providing information for everyone on workplace results is one of the most trust-generating actions that an organization can take. Not coincidentally, it's also one of the most cost-effective improvement actions available because the provided information ultimately becomes the basis of voluntary improvement activity.

Use graphics judiciously.

How should data that have painstakingly been collected be displayed? Unfortunately, those engaged in performance measurement often give scant thought to this question. The fact is, very meaningful data can be rendered confusing and essentially useless if they aren't properly presented to those who need them. Raw data can be presented as is, but once the person gathering that data determines what story is being told, the data should be appropriately processed to detail that story at a glance. This is not an appeal for distortion. Performance measurers simply have to keep in mind that statistics do for numbers what writing style does for words: they select key information and present it effectively.

The definitive book on graphical display—*Visual Display of Quantitative Information* by Edward Tufte—provides numerous examples of excellent and poor graphics and illustrates these nine rules of graphical display:

1. Show the data.

2. Lead the viewer to the substance rather than the graphic design.

3. Don't distort the data.

4. Compress many numbers into small space.

5. Make large data sets coherent.

6. Encourage comparison.

7. Show several levels of detail—from big picture to fine structure.

8. Have a clear purpose in mind for the display.

9. Integrate numbers with the word descriptions that accompany them.

Many of the common graphical errors violate at least one of these rules. For example, the scale on a graph should usually use the same absolute distance from mark to mark and should be labeled with round numbers to help the reader's eye pick up data quickly. There are several exceptions to Tufte's rules, but they should be used only for serious and not aesthetic purposes.[3]

Account for change.

Statisticians always emphasize the need for more historical data. If you have six months' worth, they might say you need at least a year's worth. If you have three years' worth, five years sure would be nice. For stable processes, the more data the better. Although science provides quite a few stable processes, they are hard to find in the world of management, where something is changing every day. For analyzing a specific process, today's change may not make any difference in the conclusion made from the available data. But when analysts accumulate small changes over days and weeks and months, it's hard to use stable scientific methods to track highly volatile trends like the ones found in a marketing or production environment.

With its emphasis on prevention and cause analysis, the quality movement has focused attention on *junction points* in historical data.

These are places where an abrupt change in data corresponds to an identifiable cause in the organization. The whole five years' worth of data may not reflect a stable process, but there may be three time periods of one and one-half to two years each in which three different marketing or production patterns were used. The different results and adjustments can be isolated and measured with some insight.

Thus, there is no overwhelming barrier to changing the measurement basis when the business changes. An organization doesn't "lose" years of valuable data by reconfiguring a marketing pattern or a machine because the data were probably inconsistent to begin with. By changing the measurement basis, the organization gains the tremendous advantage of relevance. Then current decisions can more confidently be made since current data are available for analysis.

This is not a license to change the measurement approach any time that the current measures are "misleading"—for example, when they are going down but the organization needs some going up. The measures in each family of measures should be reviewed annually. The factors that could cause change of measures are

○ New management or ownership,

○ New strategic planning emphasis,

○ New product or service lines,

○ An old measure that has little room for improvement (compared to other alternatives), and

○ New work structures (self-managed teams, for example).

When measures are changed or simply recalibrated, it's good practice to "splice" them by running the old measure beside the new measure for a few periods. Otherwise observers may get the idea that changes are being made surreptitiously.

Old Tyme Jelly: Measurement in Practice

What does a matched set of families of measures look like? Returning to Old Tyme Jelly, the fictional firm we encountered in Chapter 4, let's take a look at how families of measures are used to gauge performance at all levels.

Old Tyme Jelly, Inc.,is a medium-size manufacturer of jellies, peanut butter, and mayonnaise. The president and her seventy-five-person headquarters staff are located in Indiana along with the main plant, which produces jelly and mayonnaise. There are two other plants—one in Georgia, which manufactures jelly and peanut butter, and one in California, which makes jelly. The Georgia plant was doubled in size in 1994, at which time the peanut butter line was launched. The company has a conservative reputation, but under its new president it has grown faster in recent years than it has historically.

There is no doubt as to the top-flight quality of Old Tyme Jelly's products, but not everyone is willing to pay a small premium in price for them. The firm sells through regular food brokers for most supermarket distribution, but it also has about 20 percent of its business in gourmet outlets on the East Coast where it uses specialty distributors. Purchasing is consolidated at headquarters, with a small buying office in California and another in Mexico. The firm is moderately automated, but some of the gourmet version of the product is hand packed in containers of all sorts by seasonal temporaries at the Indiana plant. The different permanent production lines in Indiana have been organized in self-managed teams for the past two years with generally good results, but with an occasional intervention by the plant manager. There are plans to expand the team concept to the other plants soon.

The top management group bases its family of measures on the key objectives of the annual strategic plan. The 1995 strategic plan features the following corporate objectives:

○ Increase earnings by at least 10 percent.

○ Maintain market share of jelly at 15 percent, while moving to 5 percent in mayonnaise and 2 percent in peanut butter.

○ Increase shelf facings at the Red Barn and Future Dome supermarket chains by at least 20 percent.

○ Increase work-in-process inventory turnover at the combined plants by 20 percent, in spite of new flavor or new product activity.

○ Expand the use of self-managed teams from 20 percent of employees to 35 percent of employees in 1995.

○ Float $250,000 of new debt at no more than ½ percent over the London Interbank Offered Rates (LIBOR).

Although the corresponding family of measures was clear for top managers to discern, they grappled over some of the weights.

The set of measures shown in Table 12.2 lists the most important things that the executives want to have happen. The six items are presented separately, but they are interrelated. For example, an increase in facings at the targeted chains should increase market share, everything else being equal. But is everything equal? If the salesforce concentrates on the targeted chains and somewhat ignores other chains or independent retailers, there might be an

TABLE 12.2. FAMILY OF MEASURES FOR OLD TYME JELLY'S TOP EXECUTIVES

	Weight
Earnings growth (percent)	25
Market share index	25
Targeted facing footage (feet per store)	10
Work-in-process inventory turns	15
Self-managed teams, (percent penetration)	15
New debt interest rate	10

offsetting decline in market share in that direction. What is actually happening will be analyzed at the sales region level by chain and by product category. Only then can action be taken. But meanwhile, the top executives have some idea of whether their strategies are working in general.

The manager of the Indiana plant has echoed some of the most relevant measures of the top executives but has added some wild cards of his own, as shown in Table 12.3.

TABLE 12.3. FAMILY OF MEASURES FOR OLD TYME JELLY'S INDIANA PLANT MANAGER

	Weight
Plant contribution to corporate earnings and overhead	25
Work-in-process inventory turns	25
On-time shipping (percent)	15
Self-managed teams (certifications per participant)	10
Safety (OSHA reportables)	10
Scrap rate (raw material and packaging)	15

The other two plants have similar measures, except for a different measure on self-managed teams. Indiana already has the teams and concentrates on making them more effective through increasing cross-certifications. The other plants measure the penetration rate.

Thus, the top management measure on self-managed team penetration needs to be separated by plant in order to be interpreted. There is a link between the self-managed team penetration rate and the WIP data because the teams are part of a strategy to move toward flexible manufacturing, where decreased WIP is a good indicator of success.

The Indiana plant may show no improvement in penetration rate but improvement in cross-certification. It might also show a decrease in WIP, but that may not happen until cross-certification is further along. There may be increases in WIP at the other plants while they are experimenting with the new means of operating.

So each measure needs to be interpreted along with the other members of its family and with comparable measures at other levels and locations. This is management by fact: time is spent on interpreting interrelated pieces of data, rather than on expounding theories and complaining about the complexity of life.

The regional sales and marketing managers have a different orientation, as shown in Table 12.4.

TABLE 12.4. FAMILY OF MEASURES FOR OLD TYME JELLY'S REGIONAL SALES AND MARKETING MANAGERS

	Weight
Region marketing margin (percent of sales)[a]	25
Market-share index	25
Targeted facing footage (feet per store)	20
Customer-survey results (index)	20
Broker turnover rate	10

[a] Marketing margin is the difference between net wholesale selling price and plant transfer price.

Besides the issue of facings at selected chains versus overall market share as discussed above, there are other interesting interrelations in this set of measures. Broker turnover—which retarded promotions and increased the amount of out-of-stock merchandise, thereby affecting the retail customer—had been identified by some chains as a long-term problem in dealing with Old Tyme. So broker turnover was brought into the family of measures for the regions. Presumably, a decrease in turnover will be reflected (with some lag) in better customer-survey results. If not, regional sales and marketing managers will need to find out why.

At corporate headquarters, each of the major staff groups has a family of measures also. The corporate purchasing department tries to integrate its initiatives with the needs of the factories it supports (see Table 12.5).

The plants want purchasing to develop "certified suppliers." Part of the certification program requires that suppliers work just-in-

Ready, Set, Measure

TABLE 12.5. FAMILY OF MEASURES FOR OLD TYME JELLY'S
CORPORATE PURCHASING DEPARTMENT

	Weight
Tonnage purchased per department employee	25
Purchase price versus commodity quotations (selected materials)	35
Purchases from certified suppliers (percent)	25
Rejection at delivery (percent)	15

time schedules with the plants to reduce raw material inventory, which helps to reduce pressure for premature processing to make room in the raw materials warehouse for large or unplanned deliveries. Lower rejection rates also help keep the schedules clean. And, obviously, good purchase-price performance has a major and direct influence on the contribution line.

At all the plants, each operating and support section has its own family of measures. Tables 12.6 and 12.7 show two from the Indiana plant—one from the maintenance department and one from filling line number 4.

TABLE 12.6. FAMILY OF MEASURES FOR OLD TYME JELLY'S
MAINTENANCE DEPARTMENT

	Weight
Standard hours versus actual hours	25
Maintenance cost per ton of two-shift capacity (constant dollars)	30
Unplanned downtime versus total running time	15
"Emergency" work orders (percent)	20
Maintenance done by operators (percent)	10

TABLE 12.7. FAMILY OF MEASURES FOR OLD TYME JELLY'S
FILLING LINE 4

	Weight
Tons produced per running hour	20
Scrap rate of jars	20
Schedule fulfillment (percent)	30
Employee certifications	15
Changeover time reduction, selected machines	15

Avoiding emergencies and unplanned downtime are important to a budding flexible manufacturing plant because unexpected down time for a machine backs up everything to the entry door, preventing workers from continuing to independently make the maximum number of individual parts. If either or both of these indicators worsen, the completeness of the preventive maintenance program is called into question. Having operators do some of their own maintenance in some areas can greatly help scheduling and changeover time, but if the self-maintained areas are the ones showing the unplanned downtime, it may be necessary to reverse the move to self-maintenance, as illustrated in Table 12.7.

The productivity measure here—tons produced per running hour—has to use running hour as a denominator because the just-in-time plan backs off of maximum speed and replaces it with a perfect coordination target, as reflected in schedule fulfillment percent. Certifications and changeover time are related because there are goals to increase the number of people who can be on the change-over team and to reduce changeover time. It is not sufficient to have five or six people who can do a great job of changeover. Eventually everyone should be able to be part of the changeover team.

This is just a sample of the many families of measures likely to be found in an organization like Old Tyme Jelly. Each organizational unit has its own family of measures. In addition, all employees have an immediate family of measures associated with their direct work group. They are also an indirect part of the families of measures of groups at higher levels in the organization. Finally, there are measures for cross-cutting processes not found on the organizational chart, such as customer complaint handling, to which people from many different work groups belong. Each family of measures reflects one or more of the corporate strategic threads, but also includes wild card measures that are of interest only to the specific group using them.

Measurement: Not Failproof, but Worth the Effort

Measurement initiatives and systems can fail for the same reasons any business innovation can fail:

- Insufficient top-management support or resources,
- Poor communication,
- Lack of worker involvement,
- Insufficient attention paid to customer needs, and
- Insufficient time to do a good job.

But some reasons apply specifically to measurement:

- Too much top-management interest ("We want to see *all* the numbers!"),
- Insistence on a single bottom-line measure,
- Insufficient training of internal project leaders,
- Mistrust of the consultant leading the project,
- Overemphasis on specific complexities or intangibilities of the organization's work ("We can't be measured!"),

○ Dissatisfaction with results shown, whether "right" or not, and

○ Digression from key strategic threads (concentrating on the "trivial many" as opposed to the "vital few").

For measurement to generate meaningful data that will spur an organization onward, these potential problems need to be sidestepped whenever possible and squarely addressed when encountered.

Every organization is interested in finding out how it's doing. But this implies that measurement is the last step in the planning cycle, reporting results after the fact. All performance is after the fact, but the "fact" is usually part of a cycle of intermediate to further action, evaluation, action, evaluation, and so on. Measurement is a highly dynamic intervention. You get what you measure!

Measurement provides a strategic focus so that everyone in the organization understands and works toward the same goals. It demonstrates improvement quickly, so new solutions can be rolled out to other parts of the organization. It clarifies relationships with suppliers, customers, and the community, allowing cooperative activity outside the organization.

Can measurement *cause* improvement? No more than a customer focus, a strategic plan, a dynamic leader, a well-trained workforce, or good facilities alone can. But when such advantages are combined, with measures as the glue holding them all together, success is inevitable.

In essence, performance measurement is an empowerment tool. At every level of the organization, employees and managers work toward the established measures, whatever they are. This is real power! An open organization with appropriate measures will start in motion an unending improvement orientation among its workforce. And that is the ultimate success factor.

APPENDIX

☼ A ☼

National and Industry Productivity Statistics*

Statistics on productivity improvement in the United States are quoted from time to time in the press and are used by macroeconomists and national policy specialists to gauge the progress of the nation. But there are many ways that businesspeople, especially those charged with productivity and quality improvement, can use these statistics to boost their organization's performance. No information is more potentially useful than that which tells you how your industry is doing here and abroad. And much more information along these lines is available than is generally recognized. But the interested individual must search for it.

U.S. National Data

In the United States, productivity makes the newspapers and television and radio newscasts about once a month in the form of the Bureau of Labor Statistics' (BLS) *Productivity and Costs* report. This collection of quarterly data is first issued in preliminary form one month after the end of the

---

* Adapted from "Getting the Most from Productivity Statistics," *National Productivity Review* (Autumn 1990), pp. 457–466. Copyright © John Wiley & Sons, New York.

Appendices

quarter; then it's revised a month later and revised again when the next quarter's preliminary comes out. The measure is real value-added output per hour for the private business economy, nonfarm private business, nonfinancial private business, and manufacturing. It's presented only in trend form, detailing percentage of increase against the previous quarter and the previous year.

Almost none of the commentators outside the BLS get the information right, however. Aside from the confusion about which revision is being discussed, many newspeople try to make a blanket statement from the data, emphasizing performance in a particular quarter rather than a long-term trend. A statement like "productivity is at 1 percent," suggests that 99 percent of the nation is unproductive, when the correct message is that productivity has improved 1 percent in a particular time period.

The BLS also calculates an annual Multifactor Productivity Index, which is real value-added output compared to a weighted sum of labor hour and capital input idexes. It's presented at the whole-economy level and for manufacturing. Although this provides a good picture of the true economic tradeoffs in automation, the index comes out more than a year after the data have been collected, so it has limited management use.

In interpreting the recent past, it's obvious that productivity has improved more in the manufacturing sector than in the ecomomy as a whole and, thus, by inference, more than in the service industries. There is no measure presented for the service industries as a whole, so back-of-envelope calculations are made for this sector. Table A.1 shows an example that uses the fact that manufacturing output is about 23 percent of the

TABLE A.1. U.S. LABOR PRODUCTIVITY GROWTH

% Growth per Year	REPORTED		IMPLICIT
	Nonfarm	Manufacturing	Nonfarm, Nonmanufacturing
1968–78	1.3	2.6	0.9
1978–82	(0.4)	1.2	(0.9)
1982–88	1.5	3.0	1.0
1988–91	(0.3)	1.2	(0.7)
1991–93	2.4	4.7	1.6

SOURCE: U.S. Bureau of Labor Statistics (Reported); author (Implicit).

National and Industry Productivity Statistics

output of the nonfarm private sector. This, however, is partially misleading. In some parts of the output calculations, where defining the exact output or extracting the price effect from a current dollar is difficult, the assumption has been made that output simply equals labor input. Though this could be called approximately right (which is certainly better than precisely wrong), it serves to put a downward bias on an increasing index. This effect occurs in varying intensity in many but not all service industries.

International Data

In many respects, international measures should be the most useful because productivity performance levels gain full meaning only when they are compared to the performance of our competitors and trading partners. If everyone performs poorly, the United States does not lose its competitive position. If everyone performs at varying levels, it's vital for the United States to do as well as possible.

The BLS publishes an annual comparison of manufacturing productivity growth rates in twelve countries. This is heavily used because its time lag—six months—is not bad, manufacturing is traditionally where the first level of competition takes place, and some of the countries profiled are the United States' chief competitors. Obviously, most businesses would like more specific data on international manufacturing industries, but almost nothing exists at that level.

The BLS compiles, but does not officially publish, whole-economy data for thirteen countries, including the United States (see Table A.2). This represents gross domestic product per employed person, on both trend and level basis, and is the best level data routinely available.

The fact that the United States is first in full-nation productivity is not as important as the fact that the United States is competitive in enough critical industries to maintain economic health and security. But the overall national productivity statistic has become symbolic of world leadership, and a sense of world leadership is important to many Americans.

Going beyond these few countries, there are occasional data from the Organization for Economic Cooperation and Development (OECD) and an annual gross national product (GNP) per capita from the World Bank, the latter with a two-year time lag. GNP per capita is only peripherally productivity data; it is actually a social indicator, since the proportion of people

Appendices

TABLE A.2. INTERNATIONAL LABOR PRODUCTIVITY LEVEL (GDP PER EMPLOYEE, PURCHASING POWER PARITY)

Country	1991 Level (U.S.=100)	Average Percent Growth 1985–90
United States	100.0	0.6
France	94.0	2.1
Belgium	93.9	2.3
Italy	91.3	2.0
Canada	90.1	0.4
Germany	85.0	1.8
Netherlands	81.1	0.7
Austria	80.5	2.3
Japan	78.6	3.2
Norway	78.5	1.7
United Kingdom	73.4	0.6
Denmark	72.4	1.4
Sweden	68.7	0.7
Korea	43.8	5.5

SOURCE: U.S. Bureau of Labor Statistics; author (averaging of 85 and 90 PPP).

contributing to the economy varies widely from country to country. But trends in GNP per capita are useful in tracking long-term progress. Interesting energy productivity statistics for most large industrialized countries, including those in Eastern Europe, are provided by the Central Intelligence Agency.

U.S. Industry Data

There is quite a bit of data on specific U.S. industries, but most of it suffers a serious time lag or is not in the exact industry definition desired. Whereas the output of the nation or of its entire manufacturing sector is measured on a value-added basis to avoid double-counting intermediate products, most industry data are on a value of shipments basis, since relation to other industries is not at issue.

The BLS publishes output-per-hour trend for about 125 of the more

National and Industry Productivity Statistics

than 500 four-digit Standard Industrial Code (SIC) industries. About half appear in a preliminary report within a year; the other half dribble in later. These 125 are not necessarily the largest or most important industries. The BLS also publishes total-factor indexes for four special industries, including steel.

The U.S. Department of Commerce publishes the *Census of Manufactures*, the ultimate source of information on all manufacturing industries and industry segments. It includes shipments, value-added, and number of employees by SIC code, allowing reader calculation of both level and trend data. Unfortunately, the time lag is extreme—three years or more. There are similar *Census* documents in transportation, wholesale and retail trade, construction, and minerals.

The handiest single resource for industry data is the *Industrial Outlook*, published by the Department of Commerce every January, although it's not necessarily delivered then. It groups activities realistically (not just by SIC codes) and for most major groupings provides shipments, value added, and number of employees for self-calculation of productivity ratios. It fills in any lagged data with estimates, which allow at least order-of-magnitude comparison with a current date.

APPENDIX

☼ B ☼

Total Productivity Models

Frozen Standards Model (Cost Center)

This model calculates total productivity for an organizational unit where there is no meaningful information on the price at which the product or service leaves the unit. This is found most often in a cost-center plant where the sales and marketing responsibility is elsewhere or in public-sector organizations.

The starting point is a matrix of the cost buildup of every product or service offered by the organization in a base year. It separates the unit cost of each ingredient from the standard recipe for the needed quantity of each ingredient. These unit costs will typically be the actual costs in a base year but could be some kind of cost standard.

In Chapter 5, we saw the distinction between variable and fixed ingredients. Table B.1 shows a simple example from vegetable soup manufacture. Both the input unit costs and the recipe are then "frozen" and a target is established for future time periods for each input based on the amount of soup to be produced in each period (see Table B.2).

The target 1996 data are the same as the 1995 base except that they are adjusted for the expected (and later, after the fact, the actual) volume of product. The 1996 expected (and later actual) data contain 1996 costs, but they are adjusted backward to 1995 cost levels through a set of appropriate specific deflators (one for corn, one for potatoes, one for executives, and so

Appendices

TABLE B.1. VARIABLE AND FIXED INGREDIENTS IN VEGETABLE SOUP MANUFACTURE

SELECTED VARIABLE INGREDIENTS

Item	Unit Cost	Recipe per Pound of Soup
Corn	.30/lb.	.229 lb.
Potatoes	.23/lb.	.245
Cartons	.37 each	.042
Machine operators	$80/day	.0025

SELECTED FIXED INGREDIENTS

		DAILY RECIPE AT POUNDS PER DAY		
Item	Unit Cost	1000 lb./d	2000 lb./d	3000 lb./d
Plant and equipment	$500/day	1	1	1
Supervisors	$150/day	1	1.5	2
Air conditioning	.084/kwh	50	60	70

TABLE B.2. TARGET AND ACTUAL COSTS FOR FUTURE PERIODS

	1995	1996
Target	1995 input unit costs × 1995 recipe × 1995 product volumes	1995 input unit costs × 1995 recipe × 1996 product volumes
Actual	1995 input unit costs × 1995 recipe × 1995 product volumes	1996 input unit costs]* × 1996 recipe × 1996 product volumes ↓ Specific Deflator ↓ 1995 input unit costs × 1996 recipe × 1996 product volumes

*(known only on combined basis)

Total Productivity Models

on). Then, the only difference between 1996 target data and 1996 actual data is whatever difference there is in relative recipes. The ratio of target and actual recipe can be interpreted as a partial productivity index for that item, and the sum of all the targets compared to the sum of all the actuals can be considered total productivity. Some of the soup calculations are shown in Tables B.3 and B.4.

APQC Model (Profit Centers)

This model provides a bridge between an organization's income statement and physical productivity analysis. It connects change in productivity, profitability, and price recovery with each of the input factors and subfactors. The change is presented as both an improvement ratio and a dollar effect.

For any input or output of an organization, the dollar value on the income statement can be expressed as a physical quantity (or its equivalent, a constant dollar amount) multiplied by a unit price (or cost). Once this separation is made and as time passes, the data can be assembled in another direction, change in output quantity ratioed to change in input quantity (productivity improvement), or change in output unit price ratioed to change in input unit cost (price recovery improvement).

Table B.5 shows a total productivity analysis of Old Tyme Jelly. Note that four partial productivity ratios are calculated. Three are improved and one (materials) is down slightly and total productivity is up 0.6 percent.

TABLE B.3. MATERIALS PRODUCTIVITY (POTATO)

	1995	1996
Target:	\$.23/lb. × .245 lb./lb. soup × 400,000 lb. soup = 22,540	\$.23/lb. × .245 lb./lb. soup × 500,000 lb. soup = 28,175
Actual:	.23/lb. × .245 lb./lb. soup × 400,000 lb. soup = 22,540	[\$.0581/lb. soup] × 500,000 lb. soup = 29,050
		Potato deflator = 1.043
		.0553 × 500,000 lb. soup = \$27,850

Potato Productivity Improvement: $\dfrac{28,175}{27,850} = 1.012$ (or 1.2% improvement)

Appendices

TABLE B.4. **TOTAL PRODUCTIVITY (VEGETABLE SOUP)**

	1995	1996
Target:		
Corn	27,480	32,980
Potatoes	22,540	27,170
Cartons	6,220	7,460
Operators	80,000	100,000
Plant and equipment	125,000	125,000
Supervisors	54,000	60,000
Air conditioning	4,700	5,000
Other outputs	. . .	. . .
Total	583,230	655,800
Actual:		
Corn	27,480	31,800
Potatoes	22,540	27,000
Cartons	6,220	7,490
Operators	80,000	98,650
Plant and equipment	125,000	119,000
Supervisors	54,000	60,700
Air conditioning	4,700	5,180
Other outputs	. . .	. . .
Total	583,230	637,900

Total productivity improvement: 655,800/637,900 = 1.028 (or a 2.8% improvement)

But profitability is down 2.2 percent (.978) because the other component, price recovery, is down substantially in everything but capital.

Thus, the organization worked better, but the marketplace was weak. An average price increase of 8.1 percent might normally seem ample, but the average unit cost increase for inputs was 11.2 percent. The productivity improvement would have been worth $95,000 if price recovery had held, but the slippage of $508,000 in price recovery means that, on an economic equivalent basis, profitability was down $413,000 for the year.

TABLE 2.6. TOTAL PRODUCTIVITY MEASUREMENT OF OLD TYME FOODS

	1994			1995			CHANGE RATIO		
	V (000)	Q (T)	P ($/KG.)	V (000)	Q (T)	P ($/KG.)	V	Q	P
Jelly	$ 8,400	1,200	$7.00	$10,305	1,330	$ 7.75	1.227	1.108	1.107
Mayonnaise	4,800	800	6.00	6,875	1,100	6.25	1.432	1.375	1.042
Peanut Butter	2,700	300	9.00	1,000	100	10.00	.370	.333	1.111
Total output	$15,900			$18,180			1.143	1.057	1.081
Labor	$ 2,700	278.2	$9.70	$3,181	292.7	$10.86	1.178	1.052	1.120
Materials	9,500	—	—	11,400	—	—	1.200	1.065[a]	1.127
Energy	1,400	5,000	.280	1,659	5,020	.330	1.185	1.004	1.180
Capital	2,300	—	—	2,353	—	—	1.023	1.023[a]	1.000
Total input	$15,900			$18,593			1.169	1.051	1.112
Margin	0			(413)					

	PERFORMANCE RATIO			DOLLAR EFFECT ON PROFITS		
	Profitability	Productivity	Price Recovery	Profitability (000)	Productivity (000)	Price Recovery (000)
Labor	.970	1.005	.965	$ (94)	$14	$(108)
Materials	.952	.993	.959	(539)	(74)	(465)
Energy	.964	1.052	.916	(58)	75	(133)
Capital	1.117	1.033	1.081	278	80	198
Total	.978	1.006	.972	$(413)	$95	$(508)

[a] Supplied from a weighting of subinputs.

Appendices

One useful feature of this model is that it tends to separate the corrective-action responsibility. Productivity addresses the physical utilization of resources, normally under the control of the plant management. A partial productivity ratio is provided for each type of resource. Price recovery, to the extent it is under anyone's control (the marketplace can be quite capricious), is managed by the sales and marketing people on the price side and by the purchasing and human resources people on the input side.

In this example, the analytical spotlight moves right to a 12.7 percent increase in materials price that "caused" a $465,00 negative price recovery in materials. The problem may have nothing to do with purchasing. Perhaps the product development people insisted that grape jelly henceforth be made with a relatively unattainable grape. But at least you know where to start the analysis.

For a more thorough walk-through of this model, see Chapter 7 of *Improving Company Productivity* by John W. Kendrick (Baltimore: Johns Hopkins Press, 1981).

Glossary

Activity-based cost accounting (or management). A form of managerial accounting in which indirect costs, normally thought of as overhead, are assigned to projects or activities rather than to aggregations of type of cost (travel, supplies, consultants) and are apportioned by an appropriate "driver" rather than just becoming "labor burden" as in standard accounting.

Agile manufacturing. A new formulation of flexible manufacturing that emphasizes electronic connectivity and virtual organizations in addition to "conventional" empowerment and just-in-time concepts.

American Productivity & Quality Center (APQC). A not-for-profit organization located in Houston, Texas, that has pioneered many productivity and quality measurement developments, including a comprehensive benchmarking clearinghouse, a total productivity measurement model, and popularization of macroeconomic measures of productivity.

Baseline. The agreed-upon starting point for a comparison with another piece of later-in-time data.

Benchmarking. Systematic comparison of elements of the performance of an organization against that of other organizations, usually with the aim of mutual improvement.

British thermal unit (BTU). The quantity of heat required to raise the temperature of one pound of water one degree Fahrenheit. Useful in combining and comparing quantities of different forms of energy.

Capital productivity. The output of a process divided by the quantity of capital associated with the creation or modification of that output, thus a measure of the efficiency or effectiveness of the use of capital.

Glossary

Cash flow. The net pattern of receipts and expenditures of an organization, usually expressed as after-tax profit plus noncash expenditures such as depreciation.

Cause and effect diagram (fishbone). A form of diagram used in productivity and quality analysis in which systematic speculation is made on what could have caused a certain problem usually by the people directly responsible for solving the problem.

Changeover. Conversion from one state to another, in this case the conversion of a machine from one specific operation to another.

Checksheet. A record-keeping log that sorts occurrences by one or more characteristics for later analysis.

Connectivity. The ability to conduct nontrivial work applications such as ordering or product designing, remotely by computer network rather than face-to-face.

Control chart. In quality analysis, a charting technique that allows determination of whether the variation being observed in a process is within "normal" bounds or a symptom of a changed process.

Cost of (poor) quality. A theoretical comparison of the actual costs of an organization with what those costs would have been if the organization did all the right things right the first time. The gap thus defined is often compared with the organization's sales or total cost level with a surprisingly high result.

Customer. The person who receives a product or service, the focal point of the modern quality movement.

Cycle time. The elapsed time it takes to do a defined piece of work, from the receipt of all needed supplies and information to the delivery of the finished work.

Deming, W. Edwards. (1900–1994) A pioneer of the modern quality movement who emphasized the use of statistical techniques and disciplined striving for zero defects.

Electronic data interchange (EDI). A network capability where one can instantly order products and services electronically.

Glossary

Energy productivity. The relationship between the output of a process and the amount of energy required to create or modify that output.

Family of measures. A balanced collection of four to six performance measures (usually including productivity, quality, and customer satisfaction) that together provide a comprehensive view of organizational results but individually also provide diagnostic value.

Feedback. A process in which the producers of a result receive modifying information from that result. In this case, individuals and work groups of all types receive direct information about their outputs.

Fixed cost. A process cost that does not vary regardless of the level of process output.

Flowchart. A step-by-step display of how a process functions using a set of coded figures to represent different kinds of activities and interventions, used in business process reengineering and benchmarking data development.

Gainsharing. A group incentive and involvement system where the results of an organization's process improvements are shared promptly between the owners and the employees based on a predetermined formula.

Gate. A preemptive right included in a gainsharing plan where no payout will be made under certain (extreme) conditions, such as negative profits.

Histogram. A set of vertical bar graphs that demonstrates the distribution of a variable in a population.

Iacocca Institute. A not-for-profit group at Lehigh University that is the leader in developing the agile manufacturing concept.

Improshare. A form of gainsharing based on an earned-hours versus actual-hours formula, developed by Mitchell Fein.

Index. A set of numbers showing percentage variation from an arbitrary standard, usually 100, representing the status at some earlier time.

Inflation (deflation). The degree to which general or specific prices have increased (or decreased) from one time period to another.

Glossary

Input. That which is used to make an output; in productivity measurement an expression of the physical amount (or dollar value) of one or more elements utilized in the production process.

ISO 9000. A formal quality certification system created by the International Standards Organization in 1987. It emphasizes basic organization, quality policy, and mechanics rather than quality result. It is especially popular in Europe.

Labor productivity. The relationship between the output of a process or entity and the labor inputs used in creation or modification of that output.

Life-cycle accounting. A form of accounting that starts with the conception and design of a product or service and keeps the books open until all downstream costs, such as maintenance, liability suits, and "burial," are completed for that product or service.

Malcolm Baldrige National Quality Award. A quality award first presented by the President of the United States in 1988 that recognizes approach, deployment, and results of a manufacturing or service organization's quality initiative. Its basic criteria have become the standard for self-assessment of quality in the United States.

Materials productivity. The relationship between the output of a process and the materials inputs used in creation or modification of that output.

Moment of truth. In service quality applications, the point at which the service is actually delivered to the ultimate customer.

Multiventuring. In agile manufacturing, the creation of special-purpose networks involving several "virtual" organizations and individuals, their temporary integration to accomplish an often complex project, and their subsequent disintegration to avoid generating unnecessary "fixed costs" beyond the individual level.

Nominal group technique (NGT). A form of structured brainstorming where a small group of individuals from different parts and levels of an organization unite temporarily to solve an open-ended problem, in this case to create a family of measures for an organization in which they all have an interest.

Glossary

Objectives matrix (Oregon matrix). A mechanism developed at Oregon State University to aggregate a family of measures into a single performance index without hiding the component results. The performance scale incorporates a unique goal-setting capability.

OSHA reportables. Safety violations as defined by the Occupational Safety and Health Administration (OSHA), often counted to measure the safety performance of organizations.

Outcome. Downstream from output, an outcome is the ultimate result of a productive process. If the output is a high school diploma, the outcome is a job offer. If the output is a patient diagnosed, the outcome is a patient cured.

Output. The immediate result of a value-adding process, expressed in either physical counts or dollar value terms.

Pareto chart. A chart that connects frequency of process difficulties with potential cause classifications. Pareto's law suggests that a large percentage of the difficulties are typically caused by a small percentage of the causes.

Price/earnings ratio. The relation between the market price of a share of common stock and the last twelve months' earnings per share; a rough indicator of the perceived growth prospects and safety of a company's stock.

Price recovery. In total productivity analysis, the relation between the change in output price and the change in input price (cost).

Productivity. The relationship between the output of a process or entity and one or more of the inputs used to create that output.

Profit sharing. A general-purpose incentive technique where the employees of an organization receive a dollar or stock bonus based on the level or improvement of profits of their organization. Access to the bonus is often deferred until retirement, thus severely devaluing the motivational aspect.

Profitability. The relationship between the dollar value of the output of a process and the dollar cost of the constituent inputs.

Glossary

Regression. A statistical estimation technique in which functions are used to estimate dependent variables.

Replacement cost. What it would cost to replace a specified amount of old productive capacity using current design and technology.

Replication cost. What it would cost to rebuild or replace a specified amount of old assets with identical design and technology.

Return on capital (ROC). An organization's ratio between profit (adjusted to add back interest on long-term debt) and total capital employed regardless of source (debt and equity).

Return on equity (ROE). An organization's ratio between profit and equity capital.

Return on investment (ROI). A blanket term covering ROC and ROE, but more specifically the expected investor's interest rate earned for a defined project analyzed through discounted cash flow methodology.

Return on sales (ROS). An organization's ratio between profit and net sales.

Rucker plan. A form of gainsharing where the formula used is value added divided by labor cost.

Scanlon plan. The original form of gainsharing where the formula used is sales value divided by labor cost and where a suggestion system is the typical involvement mechanism.

Semi-fixed costs. A process cost that is fixed within certain output ranges but changes outside of each range.

Shingo Prize for Excellence in Manufacturing. A productivity and quality award named after Shigeo Shingo, a Japanese management pioneer, that since 1988 has recognized North American manufacturers who have made substantial progress toward flexible manufacturing, including just-in-time and related techniques. It is administered by Utah State University.

Surrogate measures. A form of indirect measurement where one relatively intangible or otherwise hard-to-measure variable, such as creativity, is estimated by measuring a related tangible manifestation, such as number of ideas submitted.

Glossary

Total factor productivity. Sometimes used interchangeably with *total productivity*, but more precisely the relationship of a value-added output to its labor and capital inputs with price effects removed.

Total productivity. The relationship between the output of a process and all of the inputs to that process (typically labor, capital, energy, and materials) with price effects removed.

Value added. Sales less purchased goods and services, or viewed from the other direction, labor plus capital plus profit.

Variable cost. A process cost that varies directly with the volume of process output.

Virtual organization. See **Multiventuring.**

Weighting. The systematic combining of unlikes, in this case (1) the combining of process outputs that have different inherent degrees of input usage and (2) the combining of the results of the family of measures members based on predetermined relative importance.

Work-in-process inventory (WIP). Process inventory located between the point where purchased raw materials enter the production process and the point where finished goods exit the production process. Measurement of WIP is a key indicator of progress toward flexible manufacturing.

Notes

Chapter 1

1. Witold Kula, *Measures and Men* (Princeton, N.J.: Princeton University Press, 1986).

2. A good source on feedback value and methods is Aubrey C. Daniels and Theodore A. Rosen, *Performance Management: Improving Quality and Productivity Through Positive Reinforcement* (Atlanta: Performance Management Publications, 1983).

3. Witold Kula, *Measures and Men.*

4. The observation that the first four letters of number are "numb" comes from Mary Blocksma, *Reading the Numbers* (New York: Penguin Books, 1989).

Chapter 3

1. The Roger Smith quote comes from Ben Hamper, *Rivethead: Tales from the Assembly Line* (New York: Warner Books, 1986).

2. The Fetterolf quote comes from Alcoa's quarterly report, Spring 1990.

3. Robert Persig, *Zen and the Art of Motorcycle Maintenance* (New York: Morrow Quill, 1974).

4. Margaret J. Wheatley, *Leadership and the New Science* (San Francisco: Berrett-Koehler, 1992).

Chapter 4

1. For information on the revolution in U.S. federal government thinking, see Albert Gore, *Creating a Government That Works Better and Costs Less*

Notes

(New York: Plume, 1993). This thinking is reflected in the following extract: "All agencies will begin developing and using measurable objectives and reporting results. . . . Agencies should be allowed to design their own performance management and reward systems with the objective of improving the performance of individuals and organizations. . . . Today, all we measure is inputs. We don't measure outputs—and that's . . . going to change."

Chapter 5

1. For more on capital productivity, see Carl G. Thor, "Capital Productivity Within the Firm," *National Productivity Review* (Autumn 1989), p. 376.

Chapter 6

1. For more on activity-based cost accounting (or management), see James A. Brimson, *Activity Accounting: An Activity-Based Costing Approach* (New York: John Wiley, 1991); H. Thomas Johnson and Robert S. Kaplan, *Relevance Lost: The Rise and Fall of Management Accounting* (Cambridge, Mass.: Harvard Business School Press, 1987); John A. Miller, "Best Way to Implement an Activity-Based Cost Management System," *Corporate Controller* (September/October 1990), p. 8.

2. Quick changeover is discussed in Shigeo Shingo, *A Revolution in Manufacturing: The SMED System* (Cambridge, Mass.: Productivity Press, 1985).

3. The Iacocca Institute report on agile manufacturing: Iacocca Institute, *Twenty-first Century Manufacturing Enterprise Strategy*, Vol. 1–3 (Bethlehem, Pa.: Lehigh University, 1991–94).

Chapter 7

1. For more on environmental measurement, see Carl G. Thor, "A Point of View: Measuring Environmental Results," *Total Quality Environmental Management* (Summer 1993), p. 349.

Chapter 8

1. For more on Shingoian waste, see Shigeo Shingo, *Shingo Production Management System: Improving Process Functions* (Cambridge, Mass.: Pro-

Notes

ductivity Press, 1992). Or, for a more readable summary, see Alan Robinson, "Simultaneous Improvements in Cost, Quality, Delivery and Flexibility," in William F. Christopher and Carl G. Thor, *Handbook for Productivity Measurement and Improvement* (Cambridge, Mass.: Productivity Press, 1993).

2. For more on team development and operation, see Carl G. Thor, *Doing and Rewarding* (Cambridge, Mass.: Productivity Press, 1994).

3. For more on cost of (poor) quality, see Wayne J. Morse, Harold P. Roth, and Kay M. Poston, *Measuring, Planning, and Controlling Quality Costs* (Montvale, N.J.: National Association of Accountants, 1987).

Chapter 9

1. For more on *poke-yoke*, see Shigeo Shingo, *Zero Quality Control: Source Inspection and the Poke-Yoke System* (Cambridge, Mass.: Productivity Press, 1986).

2. For more on measurement in a creative environment, see Carl G. Thor, "Performance Measurement in a Research Organization," *National Productivity Review* (Autumn 1991), p. 499.

3. The pathology lab tradeoff example comes from Michael Crichton, *A Case of Need* (New York: Signet, 1968).

Chapter 10

1. Good references on benchmarking are Gerald J. Balm, *Benchmarking: A Practitioner's Guide for Becoming and Staying Best of the Best* (Schaumburg, Ill.: QPMA Press, 1992), based on the experiences of IBM Rochester; Robert C. Camp, *Benchmarking: The Search for Industry Best Practices That Lead to Superior Performance* (Milwaukee: Quality Press, 1989), based on experiences of Xerox; and Gregory H. Watson, *Strategic Benchmarking* (New York: John Wiley, 1993).

2. For more on the IBM common staffing system, see Robert N. Lehrer, *White Collar Productivity* (New York: McGraw-Hill, 1983).

Notes

Chapter 11

1. A good reference on gainsharing is John G. Belcher, *Gain Sharing* (Houston: Gulf Publishing, 1991).

2. Survey data on nontraditional reward systems are found in Carla O'Dell and Jerry McAdams, *People, Performance, and Pay* (Houston: American Productivity & Quality Center, 1987); Charles A. Peck, *Variable Pay: Non-Traditional Programs for Motivation and Reward* (New York: Conference Board, 1993).

Chapter 12

1. More detail on the nominal group technique is found in D. Scott Sink, *Productivity Management: Planning, Measurement and Evaluation, Control, and Improvement* (New York: John Wiley, 1985).

2. The basic sources for the objectives matrix are Glenn H. Felix, *Productivity Measurement with the Objectives Matrix* (Corvallis, Ore.: OPC Press, 1983); James L. Riggs and Glenn H. Felix, *Productivity by Objectives* (Englewood Cliffs, N.J.: Prentice-Hall, 1983).

3. The best source on graphical display and interpretation is Edward R. Tufte, *The Visual Display of Quantitative Information* (Cheshire, Conn.: Graphics Press, 1987).

References

Christopher, William F., and Carl G. Thor. *Handbook of Productivity Measurement and Improvement.* Cambridge, Mass.: Productivity Press, 1993.

Maskell, Brian H. *Performance Measurement for World Class Manufacturing.* Cambridge, Mass.: Productivity Press, 1991.

Sink, D. Scott. *Productivity Management: Planning, Measurement and Evaluation, Control, and Improvement.* New York: John Wiley, 1985.

Index

Index

Index

Creativity, 94
  measures of, 123–25
Crosby, Philip, 113
Cross-industry study, as
  benchmarking, 139–40
Current period weighting, 86
Customer
  external, 7, 96, 102, *see also*
    Customer satisfaction
  internal, 96, *see also* Internal
    customer satisfaction; Waste
  performance measures
    concerned with, 6–7, 8–10
Customer data, source of, 32
Customer identification, customer
  satisfaction and, 96–97
Customer mix, assessing, 130
Customer relations, family of
  measures fostering, 41–42
Customer satisfaction, 9, 93–94,
  95–102
  certifications and awards
    measuring, 98–99
  community relations as measure
    of, 102
  customer identification and, 96–
    97
  customer survey measuring, 97–
    98
  direct conversation with
    customers indicating, 100
  direct measures of, 97–99
  field performance of products
    and services and, 100–101
  indirect measures of, 99–100
  market share indicating, 99
  middle management measuring,
    35
  moment of truth and, 100
  with outcomes, 101
  reorder rate indicating, 99–100
  returns indicating, 100

top management measuring, 34
  warranty costs indicating, 100–
    101
  see also Internal customer
    satisfaction
Customer service quality,
  measures of, 9
Customer survey, customer
  satisfaction measured by, 97–
  98
Cycle time, 89–90
  measuring, 9, 109–10
  middle management measuring,
    35, 36
  waste and, 108–10

Defect rate, as factory floor
  measure, 36, 37
Defects, as waste, 106
Delivery
  customer survey assessing, 97–
    98
  moment of truth and, 9
  on-time, 36, 37
Deming, W. Edwards, 135, 159
Democritus, 121
Design, customer survey assessing,
  97–98
Documentation, measures of, 126–
  27
Documentation index, middle
  management measuring, 35,
  36
Downsizing, capacity availability
  and, 107

Earnings per share (EPS), 55–56
Education, customer satisfaction
  with, 101
Employee attitude, measuring, 128
Employee commitment, 147
  see also Gainsharing

Index

Employee skill mix, assessing, 131
Employee suggestion system, 148
Employees, as performance measures concern, 7
Empowerment, 147
  see also Gainsharing
Energy productivity, 68–69
Environmental index, top management measuring, 33, 34
Environmental quality, community relations affected by, 102
EPS, *see* Earnings per share
Equipment, benchmarking, 140
Equipment mix, assessing, 131–32
Equipment use, measures of, 10
Equity, return on, 49–50
ESOP, 41
External customer, 7, 96, 102
External quality, 96
  see also Customer satisfaction

Factory floor
  control measures and, 6, 22
  family of measures and, 30, 31, 32, 36–37
  frequency of measurement and, 22
Family of measures, 13–28, 134
  authority, tools, and training needed for accuracy of, 39–40
  break-in period for, 27–28
  buy-in to, 26
  characteristics of, 16–25
  communicating, 18–19
  community relations indicated by, 102
  as consistent with individual motivations, 38–39
  controllability and, 32–33
  creating, 25–28

customer and supplier relations fostered by, 41–42
at each level, 30, 33–37
environmental quality assessed by, 102
example of use of, 175–81
factory floor and, 30, 31, 32, 36–37
frequency of measurement and, 22, 32
for gainsharing, 157
individual and, 30
information on both level and trend provided by, 22–24
for internal customer satisfaction, 110–11
internal development of, 27
launching, 28
management style and, 24–25
middle management and, 25–26, 30, 31, 35–36
nature and, 31
need for, 13–16
number of members of, 19
outside firm creating, 26, 27
quality awards criteria and, 24
receptivity to technical aspects of, 19
reward and recognition systems and, 24, 41
source and, 32
as source of positive creativity, 26
strategic plan level and, 16–17
as technically sound, 20–22
testing, 27, 37–42
top management and, 25, 30, 31, 32–34
updating, 40
weighting and, 20–22

Index

Feedback, 5, 10–11, 171–72
  frequency of, 32
  launching measurement
    program and, 28
Feigenbaum, Armand V., 113
Fetterolf, Fred, 31
Field benchmarking, 144
Field performance, customer
  satisfaction indicated by, 100–
  101
Field service contracts, 80
Financial measures, at top
  management, 31
First-pass yield, measures of, 9–10
Fishbone chart, *see* Cause-and-
  effect diagram
Fixed costs, 79
Fixed-resource utilization, 72
Flow charts, for benchmarking, 6,
  140–41
Focus groups, customer
  satisfaction indicated by, 100
Ford, Henry, 79
Frequency of measurements,
  families of measures differing
  with regard to, 32
Front-line representatives,
  measurement concerns of, 6
Frozen standards model (cost
  center), 189–91
Function points, 83

Gainsharing, 24, 41, 133–34, 147–
  62
  administration of, 156
  aggregation and, 158–60
  baseline for, 157–58
  binary terms for, 158–59
  boundaries of, 151
  capital investment and, 158
  caps and, 160–61
  communicating plan, 155–56

continuous function and, 159,
  160
custom formula for, 150
design phase of, 155
design team for, 152, 155
eligibility concerns for, 152–
  53
employee suggestion system,
  148
family of measures for, 157
formula for, 157–61
frequency of payout in, 153
gates and, 160–61
Improshare, 149, 154
individual motivation and, 155–
  56
involvement linkages and, 155
launch phase, 156
measurement system as part of,
  18–19
medium of payment in, 153
motivation and, 162
multifactor Scanlon plans, 149
profit sharing, 149–50
readiness for, 150–51
reserves and, 161
Rucker plan, 149
Scanlon plan, 148–49, 154
share considerations in, 154–55
split considerations in, 153–54
union participation in, 151–52
valuation and, 158–60
value and limitations of, 161–62
Gates, gainsharing and, 160–61
General Motors, 29
Generic cross-industry study, as
  benchmarking, 139–40
Geographic mix, assessing, 132
Goal setting
  benchmarking for, 23–24
  danger of, 135–36, 159
  see also Benchmarking

Index

Index

Index

Index

Productivity (*continued*)
  separation of from national
    income statistics, 183–87
  in service industries, 184, 185
  total, 61, 73–76
  United States industry data on,
    186–87
  United States national data on,
    183–85
  utilization ratios and, 72
  weighting and, 80–84
Productivity and Costs report, 183–
    84
Profit, contribution to, 46
Profit centers, APQC model for,
    75–76, 191–93
Profit sharing, 41, 149–50
Profitability, 43–44, 45–59
  adequacy and, 47
  before-tax basis and, 45–46
  contribution to overhead and
    profit and, 46
  earnings per share (EPS) and,
    55–56
  of individual plants or regions, 46
  net after-tax profit and, 45
  performance measurement
    analyzing, 3–5
  price to earnings ratios and, 56–
    57
  productivity and, 53–55, 189–94
  in public sector, 57–59
  of regions, 46
  return on capital and, 47–49
  return on equity and, 49–50
  return on sales and, 51–53
  of sales, 45
  on Wall Street, 55–57
Public sector
  customer identification in, 97
  outcomes and, 59
  profitability in, 57–59

Quality, 93–94
  behavioral variables and, 128–
    29
  cost of poor, 113–14
  creativity and, 123–25
  cycle time reduction and, 108–9
  documentation and, 126–27
  external, 96, *see also* Customer
    satisfaction
  housekeeping and, 127
  innovation and, 123–25
  internal, *see* Waste
  market share and, 129–30
  productivity and, 95
  safety and, 127
  see also Customer satisfaction;
    Waste
Quality awards, criteria of as
    families of measures, 24
Quality function deployment, 103
Quality tools, 6, 114–22
  cause-and-effect diagram, 121–
    22
  checksheet, 115
  control chart, 118, 119
  histogram, 116–17
  line graph, 115–16
  Pareto chart, 6, 118, 120
  scatter diagram, 118, 119

Recognition, family of measures
    consistent with, 24, 41
Regulators, as performance
    measures concern, 7
Relevance, cost and, 78
Reorder rate, customer satisfaction
    indicated by, 99–100
Replacement cost, capital
    productivity and, 70
Replication cost, capital
    productivity and, 70
Return calculations, 47–53

Index

Index

Team effectiveness
  measures of, 10
  measures of internal customer
    satisfaction and, 111–12
Testing experiences, for
  benchmarking, 140
Time, 88–90
  cost data and, 44
  see also Cycle time
Tools, for accuracy of
  measurement, 39–40
Top management
  family of measures and, 25, 30,
    31, 32–34
  frequency of measurement and,
    22
  measurement concerns of, 5
Total factor productivity, 73–74,
  76
Total productivity models, 189–
  94
Total productivity ratio, 61, 73–
  76
Toyota, 104
Training, for accuracy of
  measurement, 39–40
Transport time, as waste, 106
Trend, family of measures
  providing information on, 22–
  24
Tufte, Edward, 172–73

United States, productivity
  statistics for, 183–84, 185,
  186–87
U.S. Bureau of Labor Statistics
  (BLS), 183–84, 185, 186–87
U.S. Department of Commerce,
  187
U.S. Department of Defense, 38
U.S. Department of Labor, 86
Units, cost and, 78

Units per hour, as factory floor
  measure, 36, 37
Utilization ratios, 72

Valuation, gainsharing and, 158–
  60
Value added, top management
  measuring, 33
Verbal descriptions, for
  benchmarking, 140–41
Virtual organizations, 90
*Visual Display of Quantitative
  Information* (Tufte), 172–73

Waiting time
  measures of, 10
  as waste, 105–6
Wall Street, profitability ratios
  used on, 55–57
Warranty costs, customer
  satisfaction indicated by, 100–
  101
Warranty system, documentation
  for, 126
Waste, 94, 103–22
  cycle time and, 108–10
  defects as, 106
  excess inventory as, 107
  excess motion as, 107–8
  materials handling as, 104
  measures of, 10
  overproduction as, 106
  processing as, 106–7
  transport time as, 106
  waiting time as, 105–6
Weighting, 20–22
  base-period price, 85–86
  cost data and, 44
  current period, 86
  productivity and, 80–84
Wheatley, Margaret, 40
Whole-economy index, 86

Index

About the Author

Carl Thor is president of JarrettThor International, Inc., a consulting firm specializing in quality and productivity improvement through leadership enhancement and systems thinking at all levels of the organization. He concentrates on developing performance measurement, benchmarking, gainsharing, and award programs around the world.

Carl was previously president of International Consulting, with the Cumberland Group. Prior to that, he spent fifteen years with the American Productivity & Quality Center (APQC) in Houston, Texas, where he held a variety of positions, including president and vice chairman. At APQC, Carl led the development and delivery of popular seminars in measurement, gainsharing, benchmarking, and assessment methods. He gave major public speeches and wrote many articles, essays, chapters, and reviews on productivity and quality subjects. He was a consultant to dozens of private and public organizations.

Before joining APQC in 1977, Carl held positions in planning and operations for Anderson, Clayton & Co. in the United States and in Brazil. He also spent three years in supply planning with Exxon.

Carl is chief examiner for the Shingo Prize for Excellence in Manufacturing. He has served as the secretariat for the Network of Quality and Productivity Centers and has advised nonprofit centers in many countries. He is a director of Fundameca, the Mexican Quality Center.

Carl holds an A.B. degree in mathematics from Oberlin College and an M.B.A. in statistics from the University of Chicago. He has

About the Author

been an adjunct professor at Houston Baptist University, teaching courses in operations management and productivity. He is a vice president of the World Confederation of Productivity Science and a member of its Academy.

Carl is co-editor of the *Handbook for Productivity Measurement and Improvement* (Productivity Press) and co-author of *TQM Trilogy* (Amacom).